# Understanding
## ELIAS CANETTI

# UNDERSTANDING MODERN EUROPEAN and LATIN AMERICAN LITERATURE

JAMES HARDIN, *Series Editor*

## ADVISORY BOARD

*Understanding Günter Grass*
by Alan Frank Keele

*Understanding Graciliano Ramos*
by Celso Lemos de Oliveira

*Understanding Gabriel García Márquez*
by Kathleen McNerney

*Understanding Claude Simon*
by Ralph Sarkonak

*Understanding Mario Vargas Llosa*
by Sara Castro-Klarén

*Understanding Samuel Beckett*
by Alan Astro

*Understanding Jean-Paul Sartre*
by Philip R. Wood

*Understanding Albert Camus*
by David R. Ellison

*Understanding Max Frisch*
by Wulf Koepke

*Understanding Erich Maria Remarque*
by Hans Wagener

*Understanding Elias Canetti*
by Richard H. Lawson

*Understanding Thomas Bernhard*
by Stephen D. Dowden

*Understanding Heinrich Böll*
by Robert C. Conard

# UNDERSTANDING

# ELIAS
# CANETTI

RICHARD H. LAWSON

UNIVERSITY OF SOUTH CAROLINA PRESS

I would like to thank Leon Askin of Beverly Hills, California, for his critical reading—from an actor's and director's viewpoint—of my material on Canetti's plays and for his helpful suggestions for improving what I had written.

Library of Congress Cataloging-in-Publication Data

Lawson, Richard H.
  Understanding Elias Canetti / Richard H. Lawson.
    p.  cm. — (Understanding modern European and Latin American literature)
  Includes bibliographical references and index.
  ISBN 0–87249–768–2 (acid-free)
  1. Canetti, Elias, 1905–   —Criticism and interpretation.
I. Title.  II. Series.
PT2605.A58Z738   1991
833′.912—dc20                                                    91-13888

# CONTENTS

# EDITOR'S PREFACE

*U*nderstanding *Modern European and Latin American Literature* has been planned for undergraduate and graduate students and nonacademic readers. The aim of the books is to provide an introduction to the life and writings of prominent modern authors and to explicate their most important works.

Modern literature makes special demands, and this is particularly true of foreign literature, in which the reader must contend not only with unfamiliar, often arcane artistic conventions and philosophical concepts, but also with the handicap of reading the literature in translation. It is a truism that the nuances of one language can be rendered in another only imperfectly (and this problem is especially acute in fiction), but the fact that the works of European and Latin American writers are situated in a historical and cultural setting quite different from our own can be as great a hindrance to the understanding of these works as the linguistic barrier. For this reason, the UMELL series will emphasize the sociological and historical background of the writers treated. The peculiar philosophical and cultural traditions of a given culture may be particularly important for an understanding of certain authors, and these will be taken up in the introductory chapter and also in the discussion of those works to which this information is relevant. Beyond this, the books will treat the specifically literary aspects of the author under discussion and attempt to explain the complexities of contemporary literature lucidly. The books are conceived as introductions to the authors covered, not as comprehensive analyses. They are meant to be used in conjunction with the books they treat, not as a substitute for the study of the original works. The purpose of the books is to provide information and judicious literary assessment of the major works in the most compact, readable form. It is our hope that the UMELL series will help to increase our knowledge and understanding of the European and Latin American cultures and will serve to make the literature of those cultures more accessible.

Professor Lawson's *Understanding Elias Canetti* is one of only two book-length works in English treating the life and works of a writer whose great achievements have been recognized only late in his life. Canetti's single novel, dramas, essays, books on travel, theoretical works, and autobiography constitute an oeuvre remarkable not only in artistic terms but also as possibly (especially in the case of the multivolume autobiography) the best cultural record of the now vanished world of Sephardic Jews in Eastern Europe. He is the quintessential intellectual brought up in the humanistic and literary traditions of the Austro-Hungarian Empire, and yet he has lived since 1939 in London. Long appreciated only by specialists and a few writers and intellectuals, he was so obscure a literary figure in 1981, when he won the Nobel Prize for literature, that the press hardly knew how to place him. The *New York Times,* searching for something unique about the man, pointed out that he was "the first Bulgarian to win the prize." The London *Times* said that he was "the first British citizen to win the literature prize since Winston Churchill." In any case, Professor Lawson's study shows well why Canetti has emerged as one of the most significant, influential, and readable writers of the twentieth century.

J. H.

# CHRONOLOGY

| | |
|---|---|
| 1905 | Canetti is born in Ruschuk, Bulgaria, on 25 July, the first child of Jacques and Mathilde Canetti. His ancestors were Spanish Jews who had migrated centuries earlier. His first languages were Spanish and Bulgarian. |
| 1911 | Family moves to Manchester, England. Canetti learns English in school, French from his governess. |
| 1912 | Father suddenly dies. Mother and her three sons move (1913) to Vienna. She instructs Elias in German. |
| 1917–21 | After family moves to Switzerland Canetti attends gymnasium in Zurich. |
| 1921–24 | Family lives in Frankfurt am Main. |
| 1924–29 | Attends University of Vienna, majoring in chemistry. Beginning of interest in Karl Kraus. Meets his future wife in Vienna. |
| 1929 | Doctorate in chemistry. Translates Upton Sinclair into German. |
| 1930–32 | Completes work on novel, *Die Blendung*. Works on drama *Hochzeit*. |
| 1932–33 | Meets Hermann Broch, Robert Musil, Alban Berg. Works on drama *Komödie der Eitelkeit*. |
| 1934 | Marries Veza Taubner-Calderon. |
| 1936 | *Die Blendung* is published. It is later published in England as *Auto-da-Fé* (1946) and in the United States as *The Tower of Babel* (1947). |
| 1937 | Mother dies in Paris. |
| 1938 | After Hitler's *Anschluss,* Canetti and his wife emigrate from Vienna to Paris. |
| 1939 | Moves to London. Works on *Masse und Macht* (Crowds and Power). |
| 1942 | Works on *Aufzeichnungen* (Sketches) as a counterpoint to *Masse und Macht*. |
| 1952 | Completes drama *Die Befristeten*. |
| 1954 | Trip to Marrakesh, Morocco, with a film team. |
| 1956 | *Die Befristeten* premieres at the Playhouse Theatre, Oxford, as *The Numbered*. |

| | |
|---|---|
| 1960 | First volume of *Masse und Macht* appears. (The planned second volume has not appeared.) |
| 1963 | Veza Canetti dies. |
| 1965 | *Komödie der Eitelkeit* and *Hochzeit* premiere (*Comedy of Vanity and The Wedding*). The latter causes a scandal. |
| 1967 | *Die Stimmen von Marrakesch* appears (*The Voices of Marrakesh*, 1978). |
| 1969 | *Der andere Prozess* appears (*Kafka's Other Trial*, 1975). |
| 1971 | Begins work on *Die gerettete Zunge*, autobiography. Marries Hera Buschor. |
| 1972 | Daughter Johanna is born. |
| 1973 | *Die Provinz des Menschen: Aufzeichnungen* appears (*The Human Province*, 1978). |
| 1974 | *Der Ohrenzeuge* appears (*Earwitness*, 1979). |
| 1975 | Collected essays appear under the title *Das Gewissen der Worte* (*The Conscience of Words*, 1979). |
| 1977 | *Die gerettete Zunge*, first volume of his autobiography, is published (*The Tongue Set Free*, 1980). |
| 1978 | Canetti's plays are successfully staged in Vienna and Stuttgart. |
| 1980 | Second volume of his autobiography appears as *Die Fackel im Ohr* (*The Torch in My Ear*, 1982). |
| 1981 | Canetti is awarded the Nobel Prize for literature. |
| 1985 | The third volume of his autobiography appears as *Das Augenspiel* (*The Play of the Eyes*, 1986). |
| 1987 | A collection of notes and aphorisms appears under the title *Das Geheimherz der Uhr* (*The Secret Heart of the Clock*, 1989). |

Understanding
ELIAS CANETTI

# A BRIEF BIOGRAPHY

The son of well-to-do Sephardic Jewish parents, Elias Canetti was born in Ruse, Bulgaria, on 25 July 1905. At that time known as Ruschuk, Ruse is a small inland port some hundred miles from the mouth of the Danube and about thirty miles due south of Bucharest, Romania. In 1905 Ruschuk (which is what Canetti continues to call his hometown) contained a thriving Jewish quarter in which the Canettis, in textiles, were among the leading entrepreneurs.

In 1911 with their six-year-old Elias, Jacques and Mathilde Canetti moved to Manchester, England—not quite as pioneers, since Jacques's brother already owned a textile mill there. To join in this enterprise and to escape the patriarchal tyranny of Jacques's father were ample grounds for moving. Elias entered an English school. The boy's first language had been Ladino, sometimes called Spaniol, a relict Romance language deriving from the long-past era of the Sephardim in Spain. Second was Bulgarian, third English, fourth French, fifth—the language he writes in—German.

Jacques Canetti, an exceptionally close father to Elias, died suddenly of a heart attack on 8 October 1912 at the age of thirty. In June of the next year Mathilde Canetti, Elias, and Elias's younger brothers Nissim and Georges moved to Vienna. Here in the space of three months Elias, barely eight, learned German and was soon devoted to literature and to the idea of becoming a writer.

Before the collapse of Austria-Hungary in World War I, Mathilde Canetti and her two sons moved to Zurich, where Elias attended the gymnasium—a period to which he looks back fondly. His preparatory studies ended in 1921 with yet another move: to Frankfurt am Main, where the family was exposed to the infamous German inflation. Mob action and political murder made an impression on the mind of the future writer. But, wondered his mother, could he make a living at writing? Her doubt was instrumental in his undertaking in 1924 to begin study at the University of Vienna for a doctorate in chemistry, which he received in 1929.

More important than chemistry in Vienna, however, was the influence of the mordant satirist Karl Kraus—as well as that of Venizia (Veza Taubner-Calderon), whom he married in 1934. By that time he was a practicing writer, having appeared on the literary scene in Berlin in the summer of 1928. He associated with other writers and became a translator. In the preceding summer, on 15 July 1927, he witnessed the event that marked the beginning of the end of the First Austrian Republic, the torching of the Palace of Justice by Social Democratic workers and the police attack on the workers, killing eighty-nine or ninety of them.

In November 1938, eight months after the Nazi takeover, Elias and Veza Canetti left Austria. They settled in London in 1939, where Elias continued, and continues, to write in German. Veza Canetti died in 1963. In August 1971 Canetti married Hera Buschor, a union that has produced a daughter, Johanna.

More than limited recognition for the depth and breadth of Canetti's writing was slow in coming. He was not an unknown, however, having won literary prizes in Austria, West Germany, France, and Switzerland in the 1960s, 70s, and in 1980. In October 1981 he received the Nobel Prize for literature—not long after he had reached the halfway point in his projected four-volume autobiography. The key to the Nobel award was the versatility of his literary accomplishment, accompanied by a deep concern for the future of the human race, imperiled as never before by the threat of self-annihilation. The award specifically recognized his broad concept of the writer's responsibility in this environment.

# CHAPTER ONE

# How to Read Elias Canetti

$F$rom the brief biography above—to be expanded when we discuss his autobiography—it might seem inaccurate to label Canetti an *Austrian* writer, as is most frequently done. On the basis of two periods of residency, one short, the other more extended? There is more to it than that, and it has to do, if not with nativity, then at least with heritage and tradition and the pre–World War I role of Vienna in the Balkans. For as the capital of the Austro-Hungarian Empire and the cultural capital of Central Europe, Vienna exerted a magnetic attraction on the educated middle class both within and outside the Empire—consequently on the families of both Jacques and Mathilde Canetti, each of whom was sent to school in Vienna, where in mutual enthusiasm for the theater they met and fell in love. In this important cultural and traditional sense Elias Canetti derives from Vienna hardly less than from Ruschuk.

There is yet another dimension to the Vienna-centeredness of the Canettis. In self-interest the Hapsburg monarchs had granted tolerance and protection to Jews of the Empire who migrated there and contributed to the development—in a generation or two—of a magnificent culture and erudition, which flowered even as the political might of the Empire waned. Not that anti-Semitism was lacking in Vienna; as the Jews prospered, it grew. But because of the role of Jews in the cultural and scientific life of Vienna the imperial capital was the cynosure of the hearts and minds of Balkan Jews of the educated middle class, like the Canettis.

By virtue of some residence, then, and a large share of cultural heritage, Canetti may fairly be said to be Austrian, at least an Austrian of the old Austro-Hungarian Empire. But he is Bulgarian too. And German: he writes in German; his books were initially published in West Germany, which contains his principal readership. And Swiss: Zurich holds his pleasantest memories and is still his favorite place to visit. And British: he has lived in England for half a century, having elected to remain there after moving back to the Continent again became feasible. In short, Canetti is in a real sense, a many-faceted European: a European with an Austrian, a Viennese, background.

One highly important facet is still missing from this description. That is the Sephardic. The word derives from Hebrew *Sefard*, which simply means Spain. In the Diaspora many Jews found a refuge in Spain, and after the Arab and Berber invasion they found a mode of mutually beneficial coexistence with the Islamic conquerors as well as with the rulers of the Christian remnant territories in the north. That refuge and that coexistence were abruptly ended by the religious intolerance of Isabella and Ferdinand, monarchs during the final phase of the Spanish reconquest in the last quarter of the fifteenth century. Their insistence on an end to religious pluralism was helped along by a papal bull legitimating the Inquisition. Some Jews converted (some of those only ostensibly); many were slain; many were expelled from the country.

Among those thousands forced to emigrate were the progenitors of the Canettis. The family name was originally Cañete, a town of some importance in the Middle Ages, now fallen to minor crossroads status, between Cuenca and Valencia. The apparent Italianization of the name probably occurred as a result of the influence of the Italian commercial colony in Turkey, the place of refuge for many of the fleeing Sephardim, including the Canettis. (A simpler explanation for the Italianate form would posit a temporary refuge in Italy—possible but less likely.)

The Ottoman Turks, especially under Selim I and Suleiman the Magnificent (1520–66), granted the refugees from Spain what they were refused elsewhere in the Mediterranean world: freedom of religion and the right to own land. As a result free Jewish communities burdened by no special proscriptions as to profession or place of residence sprang up and prospered in the Ottoman realm, which then included both Asia Minor and the Balkans. Unlike the Eastern Jews, the Sephardim knew no ghettos, no ghetto oppression, no ghetto mentality (and its obverse, the intoxication of emancipation).

Canetti takes great interest in tracing the travels of his Spanish ancestors and the modification of their name to the one he bears. His paternal line lived for centuries in Adrianople (present-day Edirne in European Turkey). As Sephardic Jews they were highly conscious of tradition. In that consciousness, typically for Sephardim, they kept alive their Spanish or Ladino language, which in lexicon and phonology much resembles fifteenth-century Castilian. It was Canetti's strong-willed grandfather who moved from Edirne to neighboring Bulgaria.

Although Canetti is interested in his Sephardic forebears, his adherence to the Jewish religion is typically latter-day assimilationist: nil. But we need to observe that the route by which he arrived at this point of consensus with such celebrated Austro-Hungarian Jews as Sigmund Freud or the author/

dramatist Arthur Schnitzler depends on a different set of historical guide-posts than those outlining the path of the Jews of middle or northern Europe. Still, whether religionist or not, Canetti was a Jew in an era that saw the gestation and maturation of Hitlerism, that saw World War II and the Holocaust. One should not lose sight of that.

If Canetti is indeed preeminently an Austrian, or even if he is first a European and then an Austrian—and a Jew withal—then certain facts and assumptions of Austrian history are apt to be reflected or encoded in his writing. Probably the most important such fact in his formative years was the end of a very long period of Austrian history, that is, the collapse and dis-memberment of the Austro-Hungarian Empire, the Hapsburg Empire, at the end of World War I. In one form or another the Hapsburg realm, with Vienna at its center, had been a part of Central European life since 1278, when Rudolf, Count of Hapsburg, elected king of a shaky German realm by his fellow princes, defeated in battle the great Czech king Przemysl Ottakar II. No wonder that by the turn of the twentieth century it was assumed that the Austro-Hungarian Empire would go on forever.

True, if one looked behind the imperial façade around 1900, one would discover increasing signs of weakness: belated participation in the Industrial Revolution, economic vulnerability, paralysis and failure of liberal govern-ment, an aged and inflexible monarch in Franz Josef, the rise and domi-nance of the German Empire, and probably most important of all, the growing rebelliousness of the several nationalities—the dominant Germans were vastly outnumbered—that made up the multinational state. Hungary had been placated in 1867 by being awarded a codominant role, a strategy that only further embittered the less favored nationalities. Still, the creaking Empire may well have survived World War I but for Allied politicians such as Woodrow Wilson, who insisted on the absolute independence of the na-tionalities, and the creation of a nonviable rump state surrounding Vienna: German Austria, a "leftover country" in the phrase of the French wartime prime minister Georges Clemenceau.

The calamitous destruction of a given recurs thematically in Canetti's oeuvre, as does, above all, the question of power: its genesis, its buildup, its spasmodic climax, and its disintegration; its relation to the masses, as in his nonfictional *Masse und Macht* (1960; *Crowds and Power,* 1962). His preoccupation with the masses was given further impetus during his teen-age years in Frankfurt not only by the mob violence called forth by the ruinous inflation but also by the turmoil evoked by the assassination of the prime minister, Walter Rathenau, in 1922. Rathenau was a Jew.

5

But the one event above all that etched itself in Canetti's memory and riveted his attention on the dynamics of the crowd, of the mob, was the torching of the Vienna Palace of Justice on 15 July 1927, the event that revealed to the world the impotence of the First Austrian Republic, the "leftover state," which no longer was allowed to call itself German Austria. Canetti's primary interest in this watershed event was not, however, political, but had to do with the crowd. The following account comes from the second volume of his autobiography, *Die Fackel im Ohr* (1980; *The Torch in My Ear,* 1982), from the chapter entitled "The Fifteenth of July." Canetti, the doctoral candidate in chemistry, was living in the suburbs, between an insane asylum and a soccer field—a locale with some advantages for his interest not only in crowds but also in madness. The semester must have just ended; in any case he notes his absence from the Chemical Institute and his presence in a suburban coffeehouse, reading a newspaper's frontpage approval of the shooting of workers in Burgenland (that region of eastern Austria abutting Hungary).

In Vienna protesting workers—with whom Canetti had joined— evidently placing too much faith in the indulgence of the Social Democratic politicians, set fire to the Palace of Justice. Police gunfire killed ninety people. Responsible for the order to shoot was Police Commander Johann Schober, whose command experience dated back to the Hapsburg era. Canetti, shortly before that moment an individual person, melded himself into that crowd, and felt no resistance toward their crime. Owing to this frame of mind his memory for vignettes was especially acute. On a side street, for instance, near the burning building stood a man moaning over and over, "The files are burning! All the files!" But beside this devastating chaotic scene—the shots whipping out and the people falling—what remained with Canetti was the sense of the crowd as a dynamic entity and his place in that crowd, the individual melded into the mass. These insights, later to be elaborated on in *Crowds and Power,* never dimmed.

Canetti entered the active practice of literature within a few months of the arson and the killing at the Palace of Justice. Not that he quickly committed his experience of the crowd to paper; he did not. But he did become convinced of his literary destiny and its appropriateness (he did not practice as a chemist for even a day). His transformation occurred not in Vienna, which seemed intellectually sterile in retrospect, but in Berlin, where he spent the summers of 1928 and 1929.

Here, befriended by Wieland Herzfelde of the liberal Malik publishing house, Canetti was astounded by the intellectual openness. He became acquainted with, among others, the artist George Grosz and the playwright Bertolt Brecht. (He liked Grosz but did not enjoy Brecht's acerbity.) In the fall of 1929 Canetti returned to his Vienna suburb with a commission from Herzfelde to translate a book by Upton Sinclair, the American social reformer and later (1934) Democratic candidate for governor of California, who was the star author of the Malik Verlag. The book was *Money Writes!* (1927; *Das Geld schreibt*), a study of the American literary business, which appeared under the Malik imprint in 1930. Canetti also translated Sinclair's novel *Love's Pilgrimage* (1911) as *Leidweg der Liebe*, brought out by Malik in 1930, and *The Wet Parade* (1931) as *Alkohol* (1932). While these facts confirm Canetti's youthful command of English, they do not attest to any influence of the American liberal on Canetti, let alone on the latter's concern with crowds and power. Canetti's opinion of Sinclair was not high. As he later was to point out, in American literature Faulkner, Dos Passos, and Hemingway were then in the wings, and they represented a new level of quality.

However, the title and theme (contained in the title) of Sinclair's *Money Writes!*—most contemporary writers are bought—could hardly have repelled Canetti, for whom avarice was later to become one of his more neatly defined themes of just less than the first rank. Another important theme is stupidity. For example, in his only novel, *Die Blendung* (1936; *Auto-da-Fé*, 1946; also translated as *The Tower of Babel*, 1947), Peter Kien's housekeeper-become-wife, Therese Krumbholz, is a monster of both avarice and stupidity.

Chief of Canetti's themes—linked with greed and stupidity—is death and the necessity of beating it, of living, of surviving. This struggle, this exercise of power, may take on less revulsive lineaments than its companion themes, but we should not look for any spiritually edifying thematic complex in Canetti's fiction and plays. By the same token, conceivably happy endings are best subjected to ironic rather than felicitous appreciation. It is possible to envision a religious dimension to Canetti's theme of death and survival—death and nothingness corresponding ontologically—but this is not a dimension that has enlisted much critical support.[1]

If avarice and obtuseness are two important themes, then the third, equally revulsive, is sex. Sex rides roughshod over reason and prudence. Therese Krumbholz may have worked her way into Peter Kien's good graces by including his beloved books within her housekeeping purview, but the blue skirt that she always seems to be wearing excites even Kien's atrophied sexuality, at least briefly.

As in the case of Therese, Canetti typically makes female sexuality more repulsive than male sexuality. The excesses of the latter he seems to accept more in the spirit of the turn-of-the-century double standard. Not to mince words, he is one of the more convincingly misogynistic authors one is likely to encounter in the realm of letters. It is not our task to speculate extensively on the origin of his frequent downgrading of women. Two possible sources, or perhaps merely rationales, suggest themselves. First, a boyhood dominated by an imperiously demanding widowed mother. It was she who forced German into the eight-year-old so that in three months he knew German. She was not, however, unloving and certainly not unemotional. Second, Canetti perhaps imagines that women are more closely attuned to the realities of emotion and sex (a much-bandied theme at the turn of the century) and that if sex is bad, then women are more to blame. In any case the attentive reader should be alert to Canetti's considerable misogyny.

Thematically linked to death and survival in Canetti's works is *Verwandlung*, usually translated as "metamorphosis" or "transformation." While Canetti's concept of transformation extends beyond the man-to-insect metamorphosis in Kafka's story by that name, it is useful to note that Kafka's "The Metamorphosis" served as a kind of lodestar for Canetti, that Kafka was Canetti's favorite writer, and that in 1968 Canetti wrote a seventy-four-page essay on Kafka called "Der andere Prozess, Kafkas Briefe an Felice" ("Kafka's Other Trial: The Letters to Felice," 1975).[2] The reference is to the writing of Kafka's novel *The Trial* and to the author's letters to his sometime fiancée, Felice Bauer. We are not astounded to learn that Canetti's sympathy for Felice is in short supply, whereas his sympathy for Kafka pervades every page. There are very few writers, says Canetti, who are totally themselves. One was Franz Kafka.

Whereas metamorphosis for Kafka was—whatever its psychological implications—primarily a brilliant artistic device, a poetic device, and not only in the tale that goes by that name, in Canetti's works transformation is a two-track theme, socioanthropological as well as poetic. It is a concept by which disintegration, whether personal, general, or cosmic, may be checked and conceivably reversed—transformed.

Canetti's monumental autobiography so far consists of *Die gerettete Zunge* (1977; *The Tongue Set Free*, 1980); *Die Fackel im Ohr* (1980; *The Torch in My Ear*, 1982); and *Das Augenspiel* (1985; *The Play of the Eyes*, 1986). In that it (like any autobiography, only more so) is subjective and thus to a degree fictional (emphasis, selection, suppression), we think of it as an artistic work, an imaginative work. We have a picture of a versatile writer who has lived and written for a long while: autobiographer, novelist, socioanthropologist, dramatist, travel writer, essayist. But in what would be thought of as his prime years as a writer Canetti did not get much work published; what was published was hardly noticed by critics or by the reading public, and passed from view. That indifference stands in contrast to the reception of his later works and the revivals of his earlier works. And yet he was the same writer and remarkably consistent with himself—genre differences aside—through the decades.

In some sense then the world has caught up with Canetti. A writer who might—as happens too often—become a tiresome anachronism in his eighties is in fact very much abreast of the stream. What came between the eras of Canetti nonrecognition and recognition—if not World War II, which does offer a rationale for not publishing works in German—was the postwar perception that man was pursuing the trail of self-destruction. And that barbarism, having been contained on one or two fronts, was likely to burst forth in innumerable other places.

In considering Canetti's thematic use of death, survival, and transformation it is useful to reflect on the cultures to which he is heir as well as on two significant autobiographical facts: the sudden death of his beloved father when the young Elias was seven, leaving the boy with an abiding hatred of destructive force, and the passage of the young Elias through several cultural and linguistic environments before and especially after the loss of his father: Bulgarian, British, Austrian, Swiss, German, and French; always as a Jew, specifically Sephardic. He is heir, clearly, to a variety of cosmopolitan cultures. It would be futile to attempt to order them in terms of importance to his writing. I am only going to suggest that the Austrian (which is, or was, itself agglomerative: German, Balkan, Jewish, French) provides a model that finds frequent resonance in Canetti's writing.

It was to Vienna that the Canettis—mother and young sons—repaired after the loss of husband and father. This Vienna was a world city, capital not only of a multinational empire but also a capital of the arts. It is popular to imagine the pre-World War I years in Vienna as a period of decadence. In fact it was artistically flourishing. Its weakness was political. The Vienna to which Canetti returned as a doctoral student in chemistry in 1924 was the capital of a remnant state beset by poverty, unemployment, class rivalries and warfare, and infected with the virus of what later emerged as Austrian fascism, before it had to yield to, and then to a degree embraced, the German variety in 1938. After this, flight became necessary.

Canetti's experience of languages is paralleled by a fascination with language and languages, and this fascination is manifest in his writings. Even where he does not explicitly call attention to it, the reader ought to keep that fascination in mind and be alert to its implications. One such implication—a general one, as it happens—is that Canetti takes seriously his writer's mission of observing and of reporting and reflecting by means of language. There is very little that is brittle in either his thought or his language—which in any case, and above all in Canetti's case, comprise a unity more than a duality.

He has seen an enormous lot, having lived—and observed—almost as long as this century has been going on. Although now and again a critic will claim to have found a font of humor in Canetti, it is rarely linguistic humor—whether in German or English; in fact, North American readers are apt to conclude there is very little humor to which they can be responsive as they are to, for example, the wit of Thomas Mann. Still, Canetti's writings occasionally emit a glow of geniality. The caricatures in *Auto-da-Fé*—for example, the psychiatrist as quite likely the craziest of the characters—may evoke muffled laughter. And the magnificent autobiography, so subjective that one is caught up in it as in fiction, cannot fail to charm the reader with its confidences and reflections. But be alert; there is more to it than amusement.

If the above seems to suggest that Canetti is less humorous than he is didactic, that apprehension would be correct. But not didactic about the minutiae of bourgeois propriety; rather on a larger scale, on such issues as the survival of the human race. If man's existence, inherently his social existence, is in jeopardy, Canetti has observed the process keenly and has some thoughts—frequently obtrusive thoughts—about how a disastrous denouement may be averted.

## NOTES

1. See Hans Heinz Holz, "Elias Canettis *Masse und Macht* als religionsphilosophischer Entwurf," *Text + Kritik: Elias Canetti*, ed. Heinz Ludwig Arnold, *Zeitschrift für Literatur* 28 (Munich: Text + Kritik, 1982): 10–26, esp. 25.

2. *Die neue Rundschau* 79.2 (1968), 185–220, and 79.4 (1968), 586–623. The English version appears in the collection of essays entitled *The Conscience of Words*. "Kafka's Other Trial" will be discussed more fully in chapter 6 under *The Conscience of Words*.

# CHAPTER TWO

# The Autobiography

The focus of this chapter will be the autobiography as a literary work, that is, as it is presented by Canetti. The discussion expands the brief biographical sketch that precedes chapter 1. Any autobiography is selective and subjective. Canetti's, more selective and subjective than most, amounts to a virtual prehistory of his nonautobiographical work. The retelling of his already selective autobiography necessarily entails still further selectivity. I will try, however, to replicate authorial selectivity in a fair way. I will also comment on the relevance as well as, finally, on the whole larger issue of Canetti's pronounced selectivity.

Upon completing as much of the autobiography as has been written, the reader is apt to have the feeling that he knows very little more about the inner Canetti than he did at the outset. Lots of external facts, lots of expository discussion (in that respect like a "typical" German novel), solid erudition, interesting milieus—but little enough of self-revelation and of the wittiness that is enabled by self-revelation. Despite Canetti's guardedness, though, the very selectivity itself, the nature of the events and scenes that he does reveal, can provide the reflective reader with the pieces of an inner portrait. And who knows? That glimmer may be at least as accurate as that provided by the perhaps gratuitous revelations of a less modest, a more flamboyant autobiographer than Canetti.

If Canetti is anything but flamboyant, he is certainly not abstemious as to the volume of material presented and projected. The first volume, *Der gerettete Zunge*, published in 1977 and translated in 1980 as *The Tongue Set Free*, covers his life from his birth in 1905 (and family history beginning in the fifteenth century) to 1921, the eve of the ruinous post–World War I German inflation. The second volume, *Die Fackel im Ohr*, published in 1980 and translated two years later as *The Torch in My Ear*, begins with boardinghouse life in 1921 and goes to 1931. Volume 3, *Das Augenspiel*, published in 1985 and translated in 1986 as *The Play of the Eyes*, runs from 1931 to 1937.

Two interesting if obvious points emerge from this list of titles and dates. First, as the successive volumes march on, each one covers a shorter time span; the first book embraces sixteen years; the second, ten years; and the

11

third, six years. In light of this clear proportional progression, are we to imagine that the projected fourth volume is going to reverse field so dramatically as to include fifty-three years? Or, continuing the progression, will it embrace, say, the four years from 1937 to 1941? But at this rate the completion of Canetti's life story would seem to be anticipated at a point beyond the life span of any mortal. And that is just the point. Canetti has long identified the enemy as death and has long prevailed over the adversary. So, it would seem, will his autobiography: *Ars longa, vita* (even that of Canetti) *brevis* (Art is long, life is short).

Second, each autobiographical title so far features a sense organ: tongue, ear, eye. Each such sense organ reflects or embodies a key autobiographical detail of the given volume, as well as a more pervasive symbolism. For example, the "saved" tongue, the literal translation of the title of the first volume, is that of the three-year-old Canetti: a stranger had threatened to cut off his tongue. That his tongue was saved bespeaks the importance of language (Latin *lingua*, "tongue") to the polyglot Canetti and the writer Canetti. On a broader scale the concept of tongue/language points to the many languages spoken in Canetti's birthplace and in the Canetti household, as well as to his reflections on the origin and history of his most un-German (though, in its Italian influence, not really un-Austrian) sounding family name.

As the first volume revolves about the concept of tongue and language, so the second volume *The Torch in My Ear,* revolves—in this case almost literally—about the idea of hearing. The central chapter, chapter 3 of five, is entitled "The School of Hearing." The school has two principal classes. In the first, which describes his courtship of Veza, he learns in the course of their intellectual exchanges—which are accorded far more attention than the other components of a courtship—to both listen to and comprehend the words of others. This comprises the beginning of tolerance.

The second class in "The School of Hearing" leads to a revaluation of Karl Kraus's famous public readings, an early critical look (or rather a harkening) that presages Canetti's eventual break with the celebrated satirist. The revaluation stems from Canetti's realization that Kraus's spoken words—which, it is true, are a voicing of his written words—are originally the words of his satirized targets, that Kraus is damning his adversaries out of their own mouths. In so doing, Canetti asserts, Kraus is pandering to the innate human predisposition to intolerance. Thus tolerance/intolerance are products—or maybe functions—of the acoustically received word. The equation balances more obviously and neatly in summary than it does in Canetti's expansive treatment—which can afford to brush past the not quite compelling logic that makes Kraus's readings a pandering to, or at least a deployment of, man's instinctive intolerance.

The torch in *The Torch in My Ear* is a direct reference to Karl Kraus's long-lived journal, *Die Fackel* (The Torch). That Canetti should thus echo the name of the journal so intimately associated with Kraus might be seen as an accolade, somewhat mitigating the "revaluation" of Kraus's readings (for who, after all, relishes having his work revaluated, especially after a lapse of time?). But rather than a palliative, the title is a prediction. The title *The Torch in My Ear* really seems to say: We are going to revalue the understandings that one derives from what the editor of *The Torch* says. Which, as we have seen, is what Canetti proceeds to do. His title has announced it metaphorically.

Canetti's new respect for listening and, through listening, for openness toward others, finds convincing confirmation near the end of *The Torch in My Ear*. Here he forges an acquaintance with Thomas Marek, a crippled young man from his suburban neighborhood who is confined to a small wagon in which he is pulled about by his mother. Although the development of the Canetti-Marek friendship has its abrasive moments, its embarrassments, which at times make Canetti shy of pursuing it, in the longer run he learns to listen to Marek and to forget the dubious solace of clichés. The at-first tentative, even unlikely, relationship blossoms.

If there is a unifying theme to Canetti's autobiography—whose structural mode leans heavily toward character sketches—it is that of Canetti's learning to know the characters, such as Thomas Marek, who populate the books and who have populated his life. He eschews individual psychology; he ignores and/or scorns Freudianism, which may not, however, prevent the psychologically inclined reader from invoking it. How does Canetti get to know the characters that appear in his autobiography? We already have more than an inkling. By the sense organs that appear in the titles of the separate autobiographical volumes. First, by tongue, by the gift of language. Second, by ear, by listening—and not merely passive listening but active comprehending. And third, by looking—and not just lazily looking but by seeing.

Although the effective use of the eyes does not imply an attrition in hearing ability, the central personal connection in the third volume is fundamentally visual, and indeed with a man whose very name suggests visual perception. That is Dr. Sonne (*Sonne*, "sun"), an habitué of the Museum Café. As described in a chapter entitled "Silence in the Museum Café," Canetti, his attention attracted to Dr. Sonne because of Sonne's facial resemblance to Karl Kraus, spends eighteen months observing him. Not that Sonne remains silent. Their discussions of the Spanish Civil War impress upon Canetti that the responsible use of the faculty of sight implies refusal to look away from what is awful, like the war in question and like the destruction of the Loyalist town of Guernica, as memorialized in the celebrated painting by Picasso.

In chapter 1 above we sketched the family background and the wanderings by which Canetti's ancestors reached Ruschuk, or Ruse, as the city in modern Bulgaria is called. Although Canetti, an atheist nonetheless very conscious of his Jewish heritage, does not dwell at any length on the Jewishness of the Ruschuk commerical establishment during his boyhood, it must have been considerable.

In 1911 Jacques and Mathilde Canetti with their six-year-old son Elias moved from Ruschuk to Manchester, England. To get more breathing room, we said earlier—specifically, more breathing room vis-à-vis Jacques Canetti's father, whose patriarchal domination was evidently unbearable. Jacques had already yielded to it to the extent of becoming a businessman and joining the family firm. Elias was enrolled in an English school, accomplishing the associated linguistic feat with distinction—owing something, doubtless, to the innate linguistic precocity of a six-year-old, but probably more to his having been persuaded by his father that it was a great opportunity: a great opportunity to learn a language characterized by clarity and precision of meaning. The boy loved to read in his newly acquired language, and he immersed himself in reading and its fantasies.

Elias's confidant and interlocutor about the books was his father, the object of the child's total trust as guide to the different worlds revealed by the books. Then after one year came his father's sudden death—an apparent speedy fulfillment of a curse issued by the grandfather when the insubordinate Jacques and his family left Ruschuk for England. The survivors were Elias, his brothers Nissim and Georges, and their mother, an attractive young widow who, from the beginning in England, had felt trapped by the Manchester branch of the family. Her apparently changing feelings for her husband during their English residence did not go unnoticed by Elias, who later connected his beloved father's uneasiness about her love with the fatal heart attack. Elias also associated Napoleon with the death, for the last book his father had given him to read was about Napoleon.

The relationship of Elias, so clearly his father's son, with his mother had never been easy, and never would become so. Not that he hated her. Far from it; he admired her; but at the same time he was her dogged rival for the affection of Jacques. After the latter's death, and as Elias grew, the jealousy became not more simple but more complicated. After the move to Vienna, to Elias fell the difficult task of becoming the man of the family. For Mathilde, despite her attractiveness and no lack of opportunity—despite, then, plenty of continued emotional turmoil in her older son—never remarried.

Mathilde Canetti was passionately and eloquently opposed to World War I, which erupted in 1914. This was a difficult, even heroic role to play in Austria (Arthur Schnitzler and Karl Kraus were perhaps the only prominent literary figures to oppose the war unambiguously from the very beginning). Canetti must have been impressed by his mother's courage, which complemented his own hatred of destructive power consequent on the traumatic death of his father. Not surprisingly, then, Mathilde and her two sons in 1916 moved to the peaceful bourgeois refuge of Zurich.

Elias loved it. He went to Swiss schools, and has never forgotten the overwhelming sensation of fairness and rationality that he experienced along with his Swiss education. He offers vignettes of the teachers, different in their methods and in their responses to students, yet as a whole dedicated to fairness and to their charges—and to each other. The appreciative student, given a bit of rein to learn, remembers them in their foibles as well as their strengths but mocks or degrades none of them. The acuity of the youthful observer, the recall of the septuagenarian biographer, may seem astounding. But when it comes to observing people, the autobiography is simply typical of Canetti.

Zurich, seat of peace and stability, apparently became *too* stable, too confining for the dynamic Mathilde Canetti, who, despite (or perhaps abetted by) her intense involvement with the intellectual development of her sons, was increasingly subject to bouts of illness that took her to distant sanatoriums, where she undertook rest cures. (Sanatoriums were a favorite preserve of the well-to-do but ailing in the early decades of the twentieth century, as can be seen in Thomas Mann's *The Magic Mountain*.) In spite of Elias's attachment to idyllic Switzerland, when World War I was over, Mathilde transpanted her family to Frankfurt am Main. As in Zurich, life was lived in rented quarters—even a boarding house, the Pension Charlotte, for a while in Frankfurt—not luxurious but well within the middle-class pale.

There seemed to have been no doubt that Elias would go to university and enter a profession or business. But there was plenty of doubt about just what his field would be—and acrimony about his imputed (probably correctly) unwillingness to face up to the harsher implications of bourgeois life (like making a living) and about his preference for the supposedly soft and self-indulgent life of books and reflection and imagination. Such accusations were hard for Elias to accept, not least because Mathilde, as her husband's successor, had taught Elias as a child to revere books and their transformational potential and had engaged him in and about books in the way that Jacques had done—although surely with less consistent emotional tranquillity. Naturally enough the youth resented the change of tack represented by the maternal admonition to think about getting out and making money. Avuncular counsel too—an English uncle had been persistently issuing clarion calls to good sense, to forget the books and ideas and all that and to get serious about money.

Nonetheless, Canetti's preparatory education continued in Frankfurt. In resentment at as well as in consonance with Mathilde's not necessarily consistent values he broadened his education to include the political violence, the demonstrations, the hectic contention in the streets of Frankfurt before and during the catastrophic inflation. Like his mother he hated all manifestations of wanton power. The way in which Jacques Canetti had been taken from them contributed to that hatred, well supplemented by World War I and now the lawless violence that marked the formative years of the Weimar Republic. As he approached manhood Elias, beside harboring resentments, was more than simply sharing his mother's hatreds; he was practically usurping them. He was calling an end to her power over him. As that power faded—or, more precisely, began flickering—he fell under the sway of quite a different sort of power. He became interested in—but not subject to—the collective energy and power of the rival crowds vying for supremacy in the streets of Frankfurt. The power of the crowd was to fascinate him throughout his career.

Mathilde's power was challenged, but not yet defeated. Her pressuring was instrumental in Canetti's undertaking to begin study for a doctorate in chemistry at the University of Vienna in 1924. Although chemistry was not a field in which he had any interest or preparation, it had the advantage of providing a living in the academic or the commercial sphere. Meanwhile his devotion to books—nonchemistry books—continued unabated, and he gave his social and intellectual interests free adult rein. His mother remaining in Frankfurt, Elias shared a room in Vienna with his thirteen-year-old brother, who attended high school. It was almost inevitable that Elias should become Georges's mentor and surrogate father.

Elias crammed for his chemistry examinations, became familiar with the laboratory and lab procedures, and enjoyed social give-and-take with his fellow graduate students. After his first semester as a not very enthusiastic chemistry student he took a vacation trip back to Bulgaria—not to Ruschuk but to the capital, Sofia, where the family seat had been transferred. But back in Vienna his chief interests were the celebrated satirist and toast of the Vienna intelligentsia, Karl Kraus, and, through attending Kraus's public readings, Veza Taubner-Calderon, whom he would marry in a few years. She was a breathtakingly beautiful and intelligent woman, a few years his senior, like him an omnivorous reader and a devoted member of the regular audience at Kraus's readings, sitting always in the front row.

Karl Kraus (1874–1936) was Vienna's leading satirist and polemicist, also a literary critic, poet, philosopher, and journalist (not until after World War II did his reputation spread more widely). Initially a pamphleteer, in 1899 he founded the journal *Die Fackel* (The Torch). Early issues included contributions by European authors of world renown, but in its second decade Kraus took to writing the entire journal himself. A special issue contained Kraus's monumental antiwar drama, *Die letzten Tage der Menschheit* (1922; partially translated as *The Last Days of Mankind*, 1947), which by Kraus's estimate would have required ten nights on the stage to be produced in its entirety. Besides World War I Kraus reserved his most bitter satire for what he regarded as the corruption of the spirit by the hypocritical, falsifying use of language. He belabored the press as the prime purveyors of obfuscating, dishonest language. His method was to quote the dishonest language and then to demolish it critically, often in its own terms. This too was his forte in his public readings from his satirical works, including *The Last Days*. The readings, a one-man show, were a long-running and well-attended favorite of the Vienna intelligentsia, thus of Elias Canetti and Veza Taubner-Calderon.

The influence of Kraus's journal, of his readings, and of his politically and socially justifiable, if also conservative, tendentious, and unscientific ideas about language authenticity and ideal language stability was deep and long lasting in Canetti. He quickly accepted Kraus's judgments, which was probably made easier by the worshipful attitude of the crowds at the readings and the undoubted culpability and vulnerability of Kraus's targets. Only after several years did Canetti move away from his devoted relationship to Kraus.

Canetti's subsequent literary-linguistic concept, that of the identifying "acoustic mask," derives in part from Kraus's attack on debased spoken language. Value judgments about language are notoriously unscientific, but in fact Kraus defended the authenticity of the language of the linguistically naïve lower classes as against the willful perversions perpetrated by politicians and their retainers. Canetti's acoustic mask is a personally distinct, indeed unique mini-language that identifies not regional, social, educational, or professional provenience, but character. We will have more to say about the acoustic mask when we discuss Canetti's plays.

As to Canetti's fellow auditor of Kraus's readings, Veza Taubner-Calderon, her influence lasted longer than that of Kraus. After what would seem nowadays a very lengthy courtship they were married in February 1934. It was a lengthy marriage as well, ending only with Veza's death in the spring of 1963.

By the time that Canetti received his doctorate in chemistry in 1929, he was already a man of letters, by way of his Berlin associations and his translations of Upton Sinclair. His literary career was beginning to be professional if not exactly prolific. Not that he was ever a prolific writer. Rather, he was careful and yet emotional, extremely thorough and reflective, a scholar and a tireless reviser but also a creative writer. Upon his receiving the Nobel Prize for literature for 1981 some critics were surprised to discover that he had written only one novel, and that back in the 1930s. The Nobel Prize award, though, addresses specifically the breadth, the versatility, of his writing.

Certainly more influential on Canetti than all his doctoral studies was the burning of the Vienna Palace of Justice and its murderous aftermath. Canetti's account of this crucial event is given in chapter 1. The fuller accounts of historians lead to a fuller understanding of the arson and the murders. What Canetti omits showing is that both the workers and the government were at fault. There was ample culpability on both sides. In January 1927 in Schattendorf in Burgenland an altercation between rival paramilitary groups, usually confined to barroom brawls, ended fatally. Members of a veterans' club fired into a group of members and supporters of the *Schutzbund,* a Social Democratic paramilitary organization. Besides wounding five people, the veterans killed a war invalid and a child. The three accused were brought to trial before a jury in Vienna. The jury brought in a verdict of acquittal, despite the fact that one of the victims had been shot in the back of the head.

That is the historical background to what Canetti was reading in the coffeehouse copy of the *Reichspost* on July 15. Whereas he was infuriated by the newspaper's front-page approval of the acquittal, the Social Democrat Party establishment—consistently in charge of the municipal administration of Vienna—was ambivalent: how can a Social Democrat political establishment protest the result of a jury trial? Thus it waffled, and in waffling it failed to consult its chief constituency, the workers in Vienna. Their reaction to the verdict was the same as Canetti's, and *their* newspaper, the *Arbeiter-Zeitung* (Workers' Newspaper), did not blandly accept the verdict. Rather, the editor, Frederick Austerlitz, thinking to mollify the workers' anger, or at least defuse it with rhetoric, wrote a front-page editorial about the "workers' murderers," in which he implied that the not-guilty verdict was rendered because it was working-class people who had been killed. That kind of writing did everything but lead to a cool ventilation of passions.

Inflamed—and apparently overestimating the indulgence of their own politicians—the workers spontaneously streamed toward the Parliament and the Palace of Justice. Canetti biked the considerable distance into town and joined one of the groups gravitating toward the Palace of Justice, which had now been set on fire in revenge for the perceived mockery of justice. He did not see the actual torching; he had heard of it before seeing the flames.

The crowd at first refused to give way to let the fire engines through. A command decision was made to approve the use of firearms by the police. As the crowd, beginning to melt away, allowed the first fire engine to get through, the order to fire was given. The police fired repeatedly into the unarmed and dispersing crowd. Canetti says they killed ninety people. The actual death toll was eighty-nine, plus 1,057 wounded. Four of the fatalities were among the police.

As to the man flailing his hands and moaning, "The files are burning! All the files!" How could he be so worried about the files when people were being shot and killed? Canetti seems to imply that the derangement was crowd-inspired, and in any case not without effect: the odd lament had after all been heard. Had, indeed, been heard in more than one sense. For the lamenter became the prototype of—he became transformed into—the "Book Man" in one of Canetti's embryonic series of novels projected as the *Human Comedy of Madmen*. The "Book Man" underwent two more transformations to emerge finally as the deranged bibliophile Peter Kien, the protagonist of the novel *Auto-da-Fé*.

Canetti's account of his relationship with Upton Sinclair is not without its confusing notes. He speaks of having been commissioned to translate two books, but there were two early on and then a third one two years later. In general he is chary of detail, and even more chary of his praise for Sinclair. In fact there is none. He found Sinclair superficial—that is, in 1980 he remembered feeling that in 1930 he had found Sinclair superficial. The translation was a job, a commission that he could accomplish with four or five hours' work per day, and he was secure enough in it to contemplate translation as a livelihood. The work was both well paid and manageable, so undemanding that he could think of his own concerns while he worked. That in itself suggests no great rapport.

Perhaps another reason (we are speculating) that Canetti found Sinclair's work uncongenial lies in the American socialist author's cry for the emancipation of women. Sinclair's proletarian background—he does not as a young man bicycle in from the suburbs to join a mass movement—was about as different from Canetti's as day is from night. Although a generation older, Sinclair was much more progressive in the sociopolitical sense. It seems unimaginable that his advocacy of women's liberation could have elicited much resonance in the Canetti who was later to reveal a disquieting misogyny. On the other hand, the literary judgment of posterity is that Canetti was right in his assertion that Sinclair was superficial. Sinclair is not much esteemed nowadays, although that may owe as much to his outspoken goal of social betterment as to his presumed, and sometimes real, superficiality (which may be the prevalent value word in Sinclair criticism). Like Sinclair, Canetti is an iconoclast, but his outrage at human exploitation of humans runs more to insight and analysis than to trying to move the political process toward reform. Finally, he says nothing about Sinclair's lack of humor, although that seemed to be a shared characteristic.

The dozen or so pages that Canetti devotes to his crippled friend, Thomas Marek, are ample for the reader to grasp Canetti's misogyny, at least of that time—the mid or late 1920s. Women are either care-givers and nurturers, like Marek's docile and overburdened mother, a former milkmaid from Lower Austria who is not up to discussing philosophy; or like the benefactress whose open-ended scholarship provides financial support for the young Marek; or else sex objects, like the good-hearted but not very bright whore recruited by one of Marek's professors to attend to Marek's urgent sexual needs. The whore is supplanted by his female physician, who undertakes to double as his mistress—from which the reader is induced to conclude that she has belatedly discovered her true vocation. Authorial chuckling is all but audible, but it is not a pretty picture.

Canetti is impressed by Marek's burning ambition as reflected in his indefatigable pursuit of erudition—although rote learning looms large—as well as by his spontaneous reactions to Canetti's preoccupation with the structure of crowds. For Marek explains that if equality were a prerequisite to one's joining a crowd, then he, immobilized from the age of six, could hardly share a crowd experience. Canetti chastises himself for his tactlessness in bringing up the question of crowds. While he is sensitive to a breach of tact in the case of Marek and crowds, there is no sign of similar sensitivity in relation to Marek and women.

As is probably to be expected in such instances of boundless and uncritical admiration, Canetti fell out with Karl Kraus. The crucial occasion, in 1934, was Kraus's famous (in Canetti's view infamous) remark, "Zu Hitler fällt mir nichts ein," which means something like "As far as Hitler is concerned, nothing occurs to me to say." That can be further interpreted to mean that in view of the awfulness of Hitler and his programs the famous satirist Kraus can summon no satire. So Brecht interpreted it. Canetti took it to reflect passive acceptance of Hitler, and the damage was done. He had already seen Kraus's acceptance—a far from unique acceptance—of Chancellor Engelbert Dollfuss and the "corporate state," less charitably "Austrofascism," as a viable Austrian alternative to Nazism. Canetti did not make it to Kraus's funeral in 1936. One year later he did make it to his mother's deathbed in Paris, where she had been living with the son who was completely devoted to her and to the aura of her power, Georges, a physician.

From the installation of Austrofascism onward, Vienna, Social Democratic capital of a generally Christian Socialist (conservative) country, presented an increasingly ominous aspect. The only thing that made this period bearable for Canetti was his apprenticeship to Dr. Abraham Sonne, the durable regular at the Museum Café. Conversing with each other they discovered things that were happening at that moment as well as things that were threatening to happen. You could tell that things were bad by the unemployment figures. Canetti doesn't give the actual figures, but it was about 600,000 out of a population of approximately 6,500,000. Moreover, the same year, 1934, saw the government's armed attack on and defeat of the Social Democratic *Schutzbund* and the banning of the Social Democratic party. It was a civil war, however brief. Artillery was hauled in to shell the workers' housing projects, thus making women and children into military targets. Overall there were hundreds (government figures) if not thousands

21

of casualties. (A prominent one was Austrian democracy.) Social Democrats fled the country; many were imprisoned; nine were executed. Four months later Chancellor Dollfuss—whom Canetti loathed—an enemy of German Nazism as well as of Austrian Social Democracy, was assassinated during an attempted Nazi putsch.

Times were troublous, and two reasonable men found solace in intellectual give-and-take in a coffeehouse, one a nonpracticing chemist with three translations from English and an original drama to his credit and a substantial novel taking shape, the other a founder of modern Hebrew poetry. What were the qualities that made Sonne such a stimulating conversationalist? Canetti poses the question and then makes a number of acute observations that, as with Thomas Marek, may illuminate Canetti almost as much as his partner.

First, Sonne (described by their mutual friend Ernst Bloch as the answer to the search for a truly good man) was thoroughly impersonal. Canetti reiterates this impersonality, so that we have little choice but to accept the—perhaps ironic?—paradox residing in the equating of good and impersonal. At the same time—this may be a happy concomitant of impersonality—Sonne is utterly devoid of self-seeking. When he responds to the topics propounded by Canetti, he does so without a hint of self-seeking. And unlike Karl Kraus, he accuses no one; accusation is not his style. In his arguments he reveals a combination of delicacy and rigor, but never ad hominem denunciation.

Sonne's use of language—understandably that especially interests Canetti—is like his personal manner: it is characterized by clarity as well as firmness of diction. Sonne's diction, Canetti notes, was like that of Robert Musil in his masterpiece novel, *Der Mann ohne Eigenschaften* (*The Man without Qualities*). Further reminding one of Musil, Sonne was uninfected by the plague of psychoanalysis. A vigorous anti-Freudian himself, Canetti could only salute a like-minded confrere gratefully, for the "plague" was gaining more and more approval by prominent authors. Thomas Mann's *Death in Venice* was not the first, just the most prominent. (Mann stated in a 1925 interview that the famed novella came into being "under the direct influence of Freud.") The battle against the "plague" was all but lost before Canetti joined it.

One more point of interest in Canetti's literary souvenir of Abraham Sonne lies in the latter's manner when he spoke to women. He never did so lightly, and he did not compromise his intellect or his serious attitude. What is the inference from Canetti's description here? That one is supposed to, is expected to, take a lighter tone with women? So that they can understand? If so, the snapshot would seem to have found Canetti in a misogynistic stance—regardless of the actual stance of Sonne.

Sonne saw the war (which became World War II) coming. So, perhaps not quite so precisely, did Canetti. At any rate he and Veza left Vienna in 1938, the year in which the Nazis, with ample Austrian collaboration, effected the Anschluss by which Austria was incorporated into Germany as the Ostmark, ceasing to exist as a country or a government. At first they went to Paris, then on to London, where he has lived ever since, always returning here after frequent visits to the Continent.

# CHAPTER THREE

# Auto-da-Fé (The Tower of Babel)

While he was translating Upton Sinclair, Canetti, in a creative fervor, also wrote his only novel, eventually called *Die Blendung* (British title *Auto-da-Fé*; American title *The Tower of Babel*). Neither English-language title is a very felicitous rendering of the German—or so one at first imagines. But it turns out that the concept of *Blendung* doesn't lend itself very well to concise English. It means the blinding of a person, a bedazzlement of the eyes, thence delusion. Probably we do well to take it in its primary meaning, keeping the others in mind, and applying them all to the plight of Peter Kien, the hero of the novel.

Canetti completed the novel in the fall of 1931 at the age of twenty-six, under the working title "Kant fängt Feuer" (Kant, i.e. Kien, Catches Fire). This feat of youthful maturity is comparable to that of Thomas Mann with *his* novel *Buddenbrooks,* also written at twenty-six. A significant difference, though—comparing dates, not novels—is the promptness with which Mann's novel was published. Canetti's work did not appear until five years after completion, thus in 1936. (This date is often incorrectly given as 1935; the earlier date was when Canetti, at the insistence of Stefan Zweig, submitted it for publication.)

This delay seems to bespeak an author who could get along without much public adulation—which in fact has been the case ever since. Canetti explains the delay as reflecting his desire "to get some distance" from the novel.[1] That wish quite likely is part and parcel of his perfectionism—of his consistent conviction that the survivability of his literary work, and thus of its author, depends on its quality.

Maybe there *was* some advantage to his method. *Auto-da-Fé* received good notices, although this did not translate into popular acclaim. Even Thomas Mann, who was evidently less than thrilled at an earlier version, was generous in his praise of the published work. What kept the novel from becoming a popular success on its initial publication? First, quite likely, was its radical grotesqueness, its satire, its (then) shocking depictions of persons and events; in short, it is a "dense" novel in the best sense, but not conducive to comfortable bourgeois reading. It presumes a fairly sophisticated reader. Second, the dates made Canetti's dilatory authorial stance quite disadvantageous. By 1933 the Nazis had taken power in Germany; the proscription of books by Jewish authors followed shortly. By spring 1934 Austrofascism was ascendant in Austria. Fascism of any stripe was not a propitious environment for *Auto-da-Fé,* which was prescient in its acid satire of protofascist character types, even though it was not fundamentally a political novel.

So, with the virtual elimination of a readership in 1936 for a satirical novel in the German language by a Jew living in Austria, Canetti found most of his readers and scholarly attention via translation. In this respect he was like Kafka—conceivably his favorite author—with the important distinction that Kafka had, so to speak, a head start in German-language acceptance and a large and expanding reputation by way of translation.

*Auto-da-Fé,* ambitious as it is for a tyro novelist (most editions run around 500 pages), was originally conceived as part of a vastly more ambitious project. From fall 1929 to fall 1930 Canetti worked on what he envisioned as eight volumes of a proposed *Comédie humaine* in the fashion of Balzac—but a human comedy of madmen, or more exactly an eight-volume series of novels dwelling on madmen. There were to be eight mad protagonists in Canetti's "Human Comedy of Madmen," each to be the centerpiece of an individual novel. In an ambitious creative endeavor, guided by frequent consultation of Stendhal's *The Red and the Black,* Canetti devoted himself now to one of his mad protagonists, now to another. One finally survived, the future Peter Kien.

Kien, as we know, was not always named Kien. He was called Kant in "Kant Catches Fire," and before that he was Brand, which means "fire." To complete the fiery sequence, *Kien* in German means a piece of resinous, thus highly flammable, kindling. To vary from the fiery sequence toward greater generalization, *Kien* would be a German transcription of Spanish *quien* "who, whoever." The latter suggestion is not completely far-fetched; Spanish after all was one of Canetti's first languages. And in the play *Comedy of Vanity* a character who humbles himself into less than a human role bears the name Franzl Nada (*nada,* "nothing").

The locale of *Auto-da-Fé,* although it is never spelled out, is obviously Vienna. The time of the events is approximately contemporary, the beginning of the 1930s. The plot may be summarized as follows. Dr. Peter Kien, forty years old, is a brilliant, unattached—in every sense—sinologist. From the start we realize that he is mad, and his madness seems related to, possibly derived from, the rigorous intellectual, social, and emotional isolation that he imposes on himself. He pursues his highly specialized profession all but sealed off from the world. As far as research resources go, he can afford to be isolated; he possesses a huge private library of some 25,000 books. What world he knows is that contained in his books. They are not just his profession, certainly not a pastime or amusement; they are his life.

For eight years bachelor Kien has had a live-in housekeeper to preside over the daily maintenance of his living quarters and, increasingly, his book collection. This is Therese Krumbholz, a greedy, aggressive—including sexually aggressive—self-righteous, practically illiterate spinster of fifty-seven years. But Kien in his naïveté about people is favorably impressed by the conscientious care that she (hypocritically) lavishes on his beloved books. For the benefit of his books he is moved to propose marriage to Krumbholz. A disastrous union—and not just because of the wildly different social, economic, and cultural levels of the groom and bride.

For if Krumbholz has initially been a dutiful and obsequious servant, as a bride she blossoms in all her stupidity, vanity, greed, and hatefulness. Kien fails to consummate the ill-starred marriage, which remains a framework for the physically and emotionally destructive battles between the pair. Kien is forced increasingly onto the defensive, and the books themselves are not spared Krumbholz's enmity. She makes the eventual discovery that her husband is not as rich as she had fantasized; his funds are quite limited, and diminishing. Upon this shattering discovery she beats him up, and the unfortunate bibliophile flees his home in terror, leaving Krumbholz as mistress of the flat as well as the books.

Possessing only limited funds and lacking worthwhile contacts or sources of solace, Kien tries to enlist the help of the concierge-janitor (and ex-policeman) Benedikt Pfaff in his contest with Krumbholz. His degradation hardly mollified by Pfaff, who has already destroyed his own wife and daughter, Kien plumbs the social depths, the world—as distinct from his books. He meets up with a greedy dwarf named Fischerle in a pimp- and prostitute-infested dive called—Canetti's nomenclatural irony is not subtle—The Stars of Heaven. They develop a relationship of mutual exploitation in which Fischerle emerges decidedly the victor by gaining Kien's confidence and serving as his liaison with the world.

No longer the master of his books, his lunacy advancing, Kien gets the delusional notion that he is carrying his book collection around in his head. The hunchbacked dwarf and pimp Fischerle—whose own delusion is that he is to become a world master at chess—exploits Kien and his bank account without pity or restraint. When Kien is at last broke, Fischerle remits him to the untender mercies of the ex-policeman Pfaff, who thereupon satisfies the sadistic urges that had been thwarted since the deaths of his wife and daughter. This marks a temporary nadir of Peter Kien's fortunes, from which he is reprieved by the arrival of his brother George. Fischerle is meanwhile slain by a phony blind man into whose cup he had dropped a button.

George Kien is a Paris psychiatrist come to rescue his brother in response to a telegram from the soon-to-be-slain Fischerle, who scents a further source of funds. Some readers of *Auto-da-Fé* regard George as the novel's only sane adult, but that question is better discussed in our later examination of the principal characters. George proceeds sanely enough in his efforts to restore order to Peter Kien's troubled life and to ameliorate his pitiable condition. At the other end of town he sets up a dairy shop over which Krumbholz is to preside—and to agree contractually never to cross Peter Kien's path again. He installs Pfaff as proprietor of a pet shop next door to Krumbholz's establishment. And finally, a true savior from afar in the tradition of late-nineteenth-century German literature, George Kien reinstalls his brother among his beloved books. An ironic salvation. Peter Kien, more than ever beset by lunacy, locks the door of his sanctum, sets fire to his books, and perishes in the conflagration. From this comes the translated title *Auto-de-Fé*, with its reference to the executional burnings carried out by the Spanish Inquisition. A more direct historical model for Kien's fiery end is the torching of the Palace of Justice and the subsequent deaths. Is the fire that is the climax of *Auto-da-Fé* a symbol of anything except the end, the death that it effects, the destruction of Kien and his books? Looking ahead to Canetti's nonfictional *Crowds and Power,* whose gemination was contemporary with *Auto-da-Fé,* we may speculate that the fire symbolizes the destructive crowd, the world of Fischerle, that effectively destroyed Kien before the fire immolated him.

Virtually all of the characters inhabiting *Auto-da-Fé,* a novel often described as grotesque or hyperbolic, are themselves grotesque or hyperbolic. Bizarre is too modest a characterization; even pathological fails to adequately describe Peter Kien, although he is surely at least that. It may occur to a reader—and it has to at least one Spanish critic—that the characters of *Auto-da-Fé* are reminiscent of those in the Spanish picaresque novel of the sixteenth and seventeenth centuries, perhaps especially those by Quevedo.[2] But Quevedo goes unmentioned by Canetti, who only notes as part of his Sephardic background that the first children's songs he heard were ancient Spanish *romances.* The influence of the picaresque novel, however, is something else, and quite unlikely. What is more useful is to compare the physical deformations of the characters in *Auto-da-Fé* as a corollary, if not a predictor, of psychic deformation.

Peter Kien's physical peculiarity is his bodily dessication. He is exceedingly tall, excessively skinny, and he appears dried out—as if he lacked the vital juices of humanity. Canetti reconnoitered Vienna in search of an embodiment and found it in the person of the proprietor of a cactus shop. Further to consider is Kien's preoccupation with blindness. The title of the novel, after all, *Die Blendung,* means the blinding, and it must be that of Kien, however metaphorical, to which it refers. What blinds—besides poring over scholarly books? Hatred—a quality with which all the characters of *Auto-da-Fé* are notably suffused but which defines Peter Kien above the rest, because his hatred is not reserved so much for other individuals as for humanity in general, as opposed to books, which he loves. In other words, Kien is literally inhuman in that he detests people, whom he imagines to be inferior to himself, and loves books, loves acquiring books, collecting books, reading books. (Marxist critics, equating books with money, seize on this as bourgeois reification.)

What kind of books? Kien's catholicity of taste seems at first blush laudable. His library includes even a piece of junk with which his housekeeper and later bride feels comfortable. But in fact he eschews novels. Not novels, but Buddha and Confucius are what Kien specializes in, ancient Chinese literature, as befits a sinologist. What an obscure, what a specialized, what an exotic field! His expertise in that field, his command of the language, set him off distinctly from his fellow Viennese. Just to make sure that that distinction, that alienation, continue undiluted, Kien regularly turns down proffered academic appointments. Sharing an inheritance with his brother, the Paris psychiatrist, he can afford—if barely—to remain a solitary (read undefiled) scholar. As against human intercourse, books are his all. Even his punctual morning walks between seven and eight o'clock are not to smell the roses, let alone to mingle or speak with people; rather, carrying a briefcase loaded with his own books, he checks out the bookstore show windows, noting the growing ascendance of junk literature, which contrasts so satisfyingly with his own literary proclivities, his own search for knowledge. And as his esoteric knowledge grows, so too his ignorance of the quotidian world.

So far this Kien sounds like an older and picaresquely exaggerated version of the Zurich schoolboy bibliophile, the seventeen-year-old Canetti whom his mother denounced as more monster than man: a literary dilettante who spent all his time and energy with books, who was more attuned to books than to the workaday world. It is reasonable to speculate that the bibliophile Kien is a literary reflex of Canetti's otherwise unrepentant view of himself. But there is yet more to the Kien so far described. He is painfully punctual, he is a pedant, he is encumbered with something very like the bureaucrat mentality; and with an egoism, a hubris that precludes any trace of a sense of humor.

Peter Kien is a misogynist, which in his case means that he hates women even more than he hates men. It is a continued irony that this unregenerate woman-hater finds himself saddled with Therese Krumbholz, a woman unlikely to warm anybody's heart, a hyperbolic monster in her own right. And yet she is exactly the one who felt drawn to respond to Kien's help-wanted ad for a housekeeper, which specified responsibility and sound character, and added "money no object." A more humane, more humanly experienced employer would not have come across so coldly and patronizingly, would not have attracted a Krumbholz, and if he had, would not have been so naïve as to hire her.

We shall return to Krumbholz. In the meantime let us try—as an occasional critic does—to see Kien in a more attractive light. To do this the reader must take a less exalted view of the workaday world. There is nothing in the novel to discourage this view of the world that Kien paranoiacally turns away from; in fact there is much to encourage that view. By this reckoning Kien is barricading himself against the very real threats and temptations of the daily world. He makes himself blind, trains himself to be blind, in order to be spared having to see the awful aggression of *things* against the contemplative life. In this sense he is an Everyman, or at least every man who requires surcease from the insistent impositions of the world. But so devoted is Kien to armoring himself that he becomes sheer armor. His consequent intellectual and emotional isolation induces his madness. It seems at least as likely, however, that he has been mad from the start and that his isolation continuously strengthens it. It is his madness, amplified by misogyny and naïveté, that sets him up for Krumbholz's wiles and, pursuant to them, for the violent unraveling of his isolated life and ultimately for his death—the ultimate isolation.

Krumbholz's physical deformities add up to a grotesque caricature. Her head does not sit evenly between her shoulders but rather is permanently canted toward the right. Woodenly canted, one gets the feeling, something like the head of a ventriloquist's dummy. The picture of wooden crookedness is reinforced by her very name: German *krumm* (pronounced the same as *krumb)* means "crooked," while *holz* means "wood." Both principals then, Krumbholz as well as Kien, bear names related to wood, but of vastly different woodiness. *Kien* is a resinous, highly flammable kindling, whereas Therese Krumbholz's woodiness is crooked, distorted. The former emphasizes a quality, the latter a dimension. Their names suggest the incommensurability—that, so to speak, of an apple and an orange—which the fiction verifies.

Krumbholz's ears stick out, broad and flat. The right one, owing to the angle of her head, touches her shoulder. Thus to some extent covered, it makes the left one look all the bigger. Her facial deformity includes as well her eyes and her mouth. When she smiles the corners of the former and the latter meet on each side near her ears. She sees through narrow eye-slits. When she walks or talks, her head shakes. Her carriage is as ridiculous as the things she says. She regularly wears—with such consistency that it becomes a leitmotif in Kien's madness—a heavily starched blue skirt.

When Krumbholz presents herself for her job interview with Kien, she is a forty-eight-year old spinster. She is fifty-six going on fifty-seven when Kien, forty, to make up for her eight-year investment of time with him and to guarantee her further housekeeping service for him and his books, marries her. He has no thought of sex; he has never had any thought of sex. But with marriage Krumbholz entertains belated sexual expectations. She also fantasizes, among other things, that she is thirty. If her plight is pitiful, the reader is largely deterred from feeling sympathy by, first, her grotesque physical presence and, second, by what she says, by her acoustic mask. Canetti first set forth his views on the acoustic mask in the Vienna newspaper *Der Sonntag* on 19 April 1937; the concept applies retrospectively to *Auto-da-Fé,* where indeed Therese Krumbholz provides one of the most telling examples imaginable.

To reproduce the acoustic mask of Krumbholz's speech Canetti employs a mixture of Standard German and Viennese dialect, the effect of which, however, is largely lost in the English translation. But we can be sensitive to that part of her acoustic mask which includes her limited vocabulary and syntactic patterns. In the following passage she addresses her husband in the third person; the reference to saving Kien's life has to do with her actions after Kien, very tall and very clumsy, had fallen from a ladder in their apartment:

First a wife saves her husband's life, then she's told to get out. The man was dead. Who fetched the caretaker? He did, didn't he? He was lying under the ladder. I ask you, why didn't he call the caretaker himself? He couldn't move a finger. First he was dead, and now he grudges his wife the least little bit. That new brother would never have known. The bank must tell me. A woman wants to marry again. What did I get out of my husband? All of a sudden I may be forty and the men won't stare at me any more. A woman's human too. I ask you, a woman has a heart![3]

As befits a stupid and uneducated woman of fifty-seven, who is moreover conceited, smug, self-pitying, and greedy, Krumbholz expresses herself in short sentences redolent with cliché. Not only is her vocabulary extremely limited (said to consist of fifty words), but she repeats incessantly, for example, "I ask you" and "a woman." She has a marked propensity for non sequiturs, jumping from topic to topic in accord with her momentary preoccupations. Other favorite structures of Krumbholz are: "Anyone can [supply infinitive]" and "[supply noun or infinitive], that's easy." She has an ever-ready supply of such tired truisms as "Haste makes waste" and "Man proposes, God disposes." The real-life model for Krumbholz was Canetti's talkative landlady on Hagenberg Street in Hacking, a suburb of Vienna, but it is hard to imagine that the landlady's acoustic mask was quite as tiresome as that of Krumbholz, though perhaps it was no less revealing. Krumbholz's limited intelligence and her acoustic mask dwell solely in her quotidian world, in every respect the opposite of Kien's book-based world. The mutual opposition finds a neat summary on their wedding night. Kien obeys his impulse to lay a mass of books atop the bed-divan that is the putative site for marital consummation. Krumbholz enters in petticoat, minus her trademark starched blue skirt, sweeps the books to the floor, removes her petticoat, and makes herself comfortable, grinning. Kien flees to the bathroom and cries. They are both quite mad, but their worlds are nonetheless irreconcilable.

Benedikt Pfaff, the caretaker-security guard at Kien's apartment house, lacks the array of physical deformities to be found in Peter Kien and Therese Krumbholz. Yet he is no less mad, and on a closer look he proves to possess a number of striking physical characteristics if not precisely deformities. During his days on the police force Pfaff was known as Ginger the Cat—a reference to the color of his hair as well as to his bestial aggressiveness. We hear also of his red-haired fists, his weapons of choice; he is all for the use of his fists and considers beating to be an art. Indeed, as well as a devil figure by virtue of his reddish hair and red body hair, he is a

31

fighting machine par excellence: stocky, powerful as a bear, muscular, with short stout arms that mete out merciless punishment—and not only to lawbreakers.

With his predisposition to violence, Benedikt Pfaff has a name that is not descriptive but highly ironic. For he bears the first name of St. Benedict, the founder of the Benedictine order, the developer of the Rule of St. Benedict. *Pfaff* means "friar" or "monk." So that, allusively speaking, we should expect a religious brother devoted to the cultivation of scholarly and literary pursuits (there is a double irony here when one thinks of Peter Kien) and the abatement of sin. The real Benedikt Pfaff is a sadist, a beast, hungry for raw power, with a perverted desire to inflict torture. He glows with hatred—of women especially. He copulates with Krumbholz when Kien's absence provides an opportunity. He beats his wife and daughter regularly. A glutton, he insists on his wife's servitude in the kitchen along with her availability to endure his beatings. She dies. He then lives incestuously with his daughter, his appetite—or better, appetites—rarely sated: for food, for sex. Although his daughter's name is Anna, he insists on calling her Poli (Polly, in the English translation). In addition to the obvious psychological reason—different name, different person (thus no incest)—the misnomer recalls his presumably glory days on the *poli*ce force. After several years Anna-Polly escapes by dying of tuberculosis. Throughout these horrors Pfaff wears the mask of an upright lower-middle-class civil servant, husband, and father. A madman in a novel of madmen, Pfaff is also conceivable as a fictional prefiguration of Nazi power, which was alive and very well, if not yet official, around 1930.

As an ex-policeman devoted to the exercise and enjoyment of power, Pfaff believes in the authority of superior power, before which he is conditioned to servility. Before George Kien, who pretends to be the Chief of Police of Paris on a vacation visit to Vienna, the servile side of Pfaff's personality comes into its own. Threatened with extermination unless he leaves the Ehrlich Street apartment and Peter Kien forever, Pfaff kneels, folds his hands, implores, and proves more than ready to move to the suburbs with Krumbholz. If his pet shop should prosper and he behaved himself, owning a pub and a small circus was a possibility for the future.

Although the attentive reader will have grasped Pfaff's potentialities on the basis of his early brief appearances, Canetti reintroduces him in a much later chapter, "The Kind Father," as a congenial homebody in the bosom of his family (when he had a family), amid the comforts of the family nest. The entire chapter, as the title hints, is about Pfaff. The title also hints at irony, which is generously fulfilled when Canetti, having possibly lulled the reader into a cozy complacency about Pfaff, turns abruptly to an ironic unmasking. There were five members of the family, we read: wife, daughter, and Pfaff in three personas: the policeman, the husband, the father. Even this we might abide, at most disquieted by the sequence of Pfaff's roles. Wife and daughter share one of two beds; Pfaff has the second bed to himself. He is the breadwinner; his wife's role is to work in the kitchen, to scrub the stairs, to attend to the front gate of the apartment complex at night when the bell rings. At age ten this duty fell to Anna, to enable her to outgrow her cowardice. By now our complacency about Pfaff is shattered.

He routinely starts beating his womenfolk as soon as he gets home from work. Chiefly it is his daughter who feels the love in his red-haired fists, his wife less frequently. Both are simply objects to him, his wife for the satisfaction of his sadism, his daughter for the satisfaction of his sex drive and his sadism. Once when the meticulously allocated household finances fail to balance, both women are obliged to spend the night on the street. Such incidents hardly mar the tenor of Pfaff's domestic happiness.

As Canetti tells his story, Pfaff is first shockingly unmasked, then becomes by degrees a figure of grotesquery, and finally a caricature. That is the approximate characterizational voyage of all the chief inhabitants of *Auto-da-Fé;* the structure of Pfaff's appearances in the narrative simply affords us a more concise opportunity to see the process unfold. With the others it takes the reader a little longer to absorb the fact that the eccentricities, predicted as they are by physical abnormalities, comprise a pathological pattern.

So it is with Fischerle, born Siegfried Fischer, Kien's eventual companion and aide-de-camp—much like an earthy Sancho Panza to Kien's austere Don Quixote. Not without reason do Fischer's associates at the seedy bar and brothel where he hangs out call him by the diminutive form of his name, Fischerle. For he is a dwarf; he hardly comes up to Peter Kien's knees. Not just a dwarf, but also a hunchback: he seems to be all hump and no rump. His face, though not actually deformed, seems to echo the deformation of his body. Dominated by a huge crooked nose, it seems to lack both mouth and ears. Everything is nose—and two sad, peaceful black eyes.

Fischerle is a product of—even as he has to an extent transcended—the lower class and criminal world. To the extent that he has an occupation at all, it is that of a pimp. His wife, fat and stupid—and despite her affection for her husband evidently of little interest to him except as a source of income—is known in the dreary dive where she works as "the Capitalist." This since she had been visited every Monday for eight years by the same munificent lover. While Fischerle's acoustic mask is the criminal argot typical of such haunts as the Stars of Heaven, he has in fact educated himself beyond his environment. His head might be more accurately described as all nose, eyes, and brain. And his madness—besides resourceful thievery such as that which he perpetrates on Kien—is chess. His delusion is to become the world champion chess master, Dr. Siegfried Fischer.

To this end he fantasizes his ascent into the middle class and a trip to the United States to play the current world champion, Capablanca. How to pay for such a trip? Rob Kien. This is apparent early on when, playing on his own surname, Fischerle denotes himself as the fisherman and Kien as the fish, the catch. The fraud involves Fischerle's ingratiating himself with Kien and over time converting the latter's books into money. A con game, a swindle. Fischerle is astute, and the game is played in his, not Kien's world. And Kien is anything but astute when he is out of his own world—which he now is, having fled Krumbholz and locked her in the flat. Is Canetti, Jewish, playing on the dangerous field of racial stereotyping, with whatever irony, when he appears to be signaling Fischerle's acquisitiveness not only by his hump—like that of a camel that has stored up food and water—but also by his large Jewish nose? Fischerle's slightly bent fingers are probably equally indicative of acquisitiveness, but race neutral.

How does Kien get into Fischerle's world? After three weeks of freedom from Krumbholz, during which he has explored every bookshop in town, Kien, lonely, wanders into the Stars of Heaven. Appalled by the filth and the cries for help issuing from remote alcoves, he is nursing a coffee when Fischerle's hump comes into view. Petulantly—Fischerle is habitually petulant—he asserts himself to Kien, maneuvers him into a closer relationship. After a while Kien invites the dwarf to enter his service, which is exactly what Fischerle wants.

Here two analogues of the Fischerle/Kien relationship suggest themselves. First, already mentioned, is that of Sancho Panza and Quixote. A squire from the lower classes, ambitious, lower in stature as well as in social class, dependent upon his master's resources, takes service with an austere master, relatively well-to-do, ripe for adventure. Further, a master who has been addled by books. And still further—since nomenclature in *Auto-da-Fé* seems to be more than casually relevant—both masters share the same phoneme at the beginning of their names: *Quixote/Kien*.

The second analogue of Fischerle is the picaro, the rogue figure that finds its most celebrated development in episodic Spanish novels of the sixteenth and seventeenth centuries, for example, *Lazarillo de Tormes* and Francisco de Quevedo's *La vida del Buscón. (Auto-da-Fé* is also largely episodic in structure.) The picaro is an adventurous, tricky young man of the lower class, wise—or who becomes wise—in the ways of the world, eager to advance his well-being by cheating and conning the representatives of the bourgeois world, with whom he may profitably ally himself. His goal has nothing to do with class equality, however, and his apprenticeship is likely to be served among those who are, like himself, in the semicriminal (or out right criminal) reaches of the lowest level of society.

Fischerle qualifies as a picaro. Despite occasional recourse to sentimentalism—those sad and tranquil black eyes—he is an unregenerate crook who instinctively spots the main chance in the vulnerable Kien, who—to carry the fisherman/fish metaphor a half-step further—is not just a fish, but a fish out of water, ready to be cleaned, so to speak. There is one further suggestive hint of Fischerle's picaresque authenticity. In *Lazarillo de Tormes*, the oldest, prototypical Spanish picaresque novel, the eponymous hero makes sport and profit out of victimizing his first master, a blind beggar. Peter Kien lives in fear of going blind, of suffering a blinding, that is, a *Blendung*.

While such details are tantalizing, they clearly do not vouch for anything like a direct influence of the Spanish picaresque novel on *Auto-da-Fé*. Many novels are episodic, and many characters are picaresque to a greater or lesser degree. Canetti mentions no picaresque antecedents, from which we may take it that he did not consciously rely on a tradition that, however, he could hardly have been totally unaware of. Let us say only that the picaresque tradition provides an extra dimension in understanding his novel.

How does Fischerle clean out his unwitting benefactor? He contrives to take advantage of Kien's disorientation—out in the real, lower-class world—and his bibliophilism. The dwarf hires four of his cronies at slave wages to tempt Kien, each in turn, with a package supposedly containing learned and valuable books for a price of several hundred schillings. Actually these packages contain junk literature purchased at a nearby bookshop for twenty schillings. Kien, the book-lover, is to be encountered on the seventh floor of the Theresianum, that part of the national pawnshop given over to the pawning of books. When Kien moves to take the wrapper from the package, Fischerle's crooked cohort is supposed to seize the package and take it back to Fischerle for reuse. In this fraudulent fashion the dwarf accumulates his patron's dwindling fortune. With the proceeds he purchases a fashionable, slightly outré wardrobe, including a suit jacket that perfectly conceals his hump, as well as a fake passport and passage to America. Unfortunately, when he stops by his quarters at the Stars of Heaven he is murdered by the phony blind man, who is in bed with the Capitalist. Murdered not for reasons of passion but because Fischerle had the unwisdom earlier to deposit a button in his cup. Not only murdered, but his hump sliced off. What the new suit did not have much of an opportunity to do— rid Fischerle of his prime physical deformity—the bread knife does.

The fifth of the five principal characters is George Kien, the psychiatrist brother of Peter. George dominates the final third of the novel. The narrative focus shifts and dwells on him in a somewhat airy fashion that recent criticism has on the whole come to see as largely ironic. The older consensus was that George Kien is the only sane character in a narrative landscape of madmen. The occasional revisionist view that George is perhaps the craziest of them all is more clever than strictly true, but it helps suggest the range within which it is possible to place this redoubtable psychiatrist from Paris who so efficiently dispatches Therese Krumbholz and Benedikt Pfaff to suburban entrepreneurship and who restores Peter, however temporarily, to his library—complete with the return of the pawned books.

That all may not be quite so tidy in the apparent restoration of the status quo—and was the status quo in any case desirable?—may be suggested by the reminder that it was Fischerle's forged telegram that had pried George loose from his devoted inmates (whose devotion he more than returned). Third, it is George Kien who suggests the fiery suicide to his too-suggestible brother. Having declared the unimportance of women through a parabolic description of termites that thrive with very few females and in their suicidal swarming release their amassed sexuality, George continues: "It [the mad swarming] is as if . . . you were to set fire to yourself and all your books" (433). True, George later regrets his suggestive metaphor, but the damage has been done.

Unlike his brother, unlike Pfaff and Krumbholz and Fischerle, George Kien has no physical deformities or peculiarities. Quite the contrary; he is handsome, tall, and strong. His features are gentle, his facial muscles mobile. His appearance evokes the Adam of Michelangelo. George's flaws are solely those of the spirit; he is cold, calculating, inhumane—despite the devotion of his mentally unbalanced patients—and a farceur. It is no wonder that Peter doesn't like him and distrusts him. But that easy formulation trivializes a profound sibling rivalry dating from childhood, in which Peter, the older, had thoroughly dominated his younger brother. Far from being a genuine hero to the rescue, George sets up the conditions for the final fraternal calamity.

It is instructive to consider the questionable method by which George was elevated to the directorship of the asylum in Paris, which he had effectively been running from his post as assistant. Upon the former director's being poisoned by his wife, George, in full knowledge of what had happened, makes the widow his own third wife and succeeds to the directorship. In this post he rejects the traditional (Freudian) psychiatry of his slain predecessor. To say the least, George is manipulative and power hungry.

Opportunistic too. Always a womanizer and proud of his professed ability to "read" women, George had been a socialite gynecologist before turning to psychiatry. His change of specialty is occasioned by a fortuitous meeting with the "gorilla," actually a madman in a gorilla suit, brother of a wealthy banker, who keeps him in a villa. The gorilla, inventor of his own language—his own acoustic mask?—is just the antidote for George's state of alienation. Fascinated, George becomes a vitalist and rejects the over-refined, vapid civilization that he had formerly so enjoyed. Freed at last from the suffocating rational dominance—at long distance—of his brother, George returns to childhood to learn the language of emotion.

It does not take long for George to exploit his new antirational ideology. He publishes an essay on the language of the gorilla; he rejects literature, of which he had been a devotee; he conceives an admiration of the insane. His mission, as he sees it, is not to cure them but to learn from them, from their inability to sustain their own identity. He is convinced that the aetiology of madness lies in the effect of the crowd, the "mass-soul" within them. The one real motivating force is the human compulsion to be incorporated into the mass. Here Canetti incorporates his ideas about the crowd, later expressed in *Crowds and Power,* into the fiction of *Auto-da-Fé.* In the present instance it makes for an enervating tension, subsumed as it is in the thought of the defamed George Kien.

The implications of George's newly insightful relationship with his mentally ill patients is that they are to be kept like a troupe of adoring animals, pets, permanently sustaining the director's vitalistic conceits. When he formerly devoted himself to cures or remissions, patients became merely banal, normal, after recovery. Now, they remain interesting, peculiar, unique, as he uses them to assuage his own devils, those related to the dominance of his older brother. It is evidently a psychologically more profitable exploitation than that of women, which formerly occupied him. It is interesting to see that both come into play in the "rescue" of his brother. George Kien manipulates Pfaff and Krumbholz with fine discernment.

In all of *Auto-da-Fé* the only sane character of even secondary importance is the engaging schoolboy whom we meet at the very outset, the nine-year-old Franz Metzger. His role is brief but important, that of introducing the reader to the sinologist Peter Kien. The introduction is effected in two pages of dramatic dialogue—no exposition—outside a bookstore show window. There Kien, on his morning walk, comes across the boy looking in the window on his way to school. To Kien's question, Which would he rather have, a piece of chocolate or a book? Franz replies: a book.

About forty words into the novel, then, the reader is confronted with a thematic revelation: a world oriented to books versus a world oriented to materialism. He is also confronted with a genial and chatty, sympathetic Peter Kien, drawn to a boy who likes books. It emerges in their conversation that Franz knows about China and the Great Wall; he would like to go to school there. He informs Kien that the Chinese have forty thousand letters in their alphabet. When Kien extracts a book from his briefcase, Franz identifies the writing as Chinese, although he had not previously seen a Chinese book. Kien, pedantically enough, identifies two of the characters as standing for Meng Tse, the philosopher who lived 2,250 years ago. Can Franz remember that? And the boy does so, correctly answering Kien's question a bit later.

Franz Metzger, like Pfaff, like Kien, like Krumbholz-Kien, lives in the complex at 24 Ehrlich Street. He knows Kien by sight, but he observes that Kien always looks away. He knows that Kien is called Professor but in fact has no academic appointment, and that Kien has a library. The boy, when he grows up, intends to have a library. He enthusiastically accepts an invitation to visit Kien's library—could it be this very afternoon? No, Kien puts him off; not before a week. (In good faith Franz shows up, only to be refused and rebuffed by Krumbholz.)

The two-page dialogue has revealed almost as much about Kien as about Franz Metzger—even if it has led the reader to imagine a more gregarious and approachable Kien than later facts substantiate. Indeed, no sooner had Franz gone along to school than Kien wonders why, against his habit, he had let himself in for a conversation that he was not obliged to undertake. Although the reader may at first wonder too, he can in retrospect be sure. It was, first, because Franz has awakened Kien's memories of his own childhood—he sees in Franz a picture of what he himself had been some thirty-one years ago. And second, with a certain proselytizing glow, he realizes that Franz could become a future sinologist. A bit later we learn that Kien is a bachelor; then, that he remains celibate when married; the point here is that he is most unlikely to father a son to succeed himself. This last, fundamentally egotistic, even exploitive point of view has something in common with his brother George's exploitation of patients for his own psychological comfort.

From such details as the above and from the relation to the novel of the brief episode involving Franz Metzger, one gains the impression that *Auto-da-Fé* is a structurally coherent whole. As we shall shortly see, Canetti evidently took no small pains to make it so. And yet he was not entirely successful. Much of it remains episodic, some of it only dubiously related to the whole, imperfectly integrated.

The novel is divided, first, into three parts bearing the cryptic titles "A Head without a World," "Headless World," and "The World in the Head." The head referred to is that of Peter Kien, and it is helpful for the reader to imagine the titles of the three parts as well as the chapter titles as having been conceived by Peter Kien—helpful because it focuses our point of view parallel with his. As a logical analysis of the titles of the parts would suggest, the three parts are dissimilar. Dissimilar, as it turns out, not only in narrative content but also as to the degree of successful presentation.

Part 1, "A Head without a World," is homogenous. Its fourteen chapters, each in itself a complete narrative with its own symbolic title, are united by the presence of Kien, the protagonist, and Krumbholz, his antagonist. Other characters, such as the boy Franz Metzger, are secondary. Kien, who is all head, all intellect, a genius of memory, is ignorant of the world—or the "real world," as it is nowadays called. The head, Kien, is bereft of the world, is "without a world." And at the end of the first part Kien is expelled by his wife, the former Therese Krumbholz, from his flat, from his library, and thrust into the world. Frustrated by his sexual indifference, his allegiance to his cerebration, to his library, and by his unwillingness to relinquish his bankbook, whose balance is much less than she fantasizes, she beats him up and throws him out—with the bankbook in his pocket.

Part 1 is a straightforward narrative occasionally punctuated by dramatic scenes such as the opening, in which dialogue between Kien and Franz Metzger runs without interruption for two pages, or in verbal exchanges between Kien and Krumbholz, without exposition. The latter exchanges are shorter because Krumbholz's verbal resources are more limited than those of the nine-year-old boy. The domestic dialogues are seamlessly integrated into the ongoing narration. And each chapter is a fully worked-out narrative as well as an integrated subdivision of the larger narration, the part.

Part 2, "Headless World," consists of ten chapters dwelling on Kien's entering a world conspicuously lacking the cerebral values that he cherishes and represents. Its values are—Krumbholz has already set the tone—ambition, egoism, and love of money. Kien is to be pitied trying to make his uncomprehending way through this jungle. Here Fischerle stands out; he and Kien form an unlikely if inseparable pair until the former's flight to America is aborted by his murder. And they do have an important quality in common: both are dreamers. But in an appropriate reflection of the travails of the headless world, Fischerle's practical wisdom—how to beat the game on the ugly streets—brings about the loss of Kien's books and his economic ruination. His mental and then physical ruination feature a hallucination of murdering Krumbholz, and then getting beat up by Pfaff and Krumbholz (with whom Pfaff has moved in). The fight and the consequent outrageous charge that Kien is a thief lead to a grotesque scene in the police station that thoroughly debunks the notion of justice. (The chapter entitled "The Thief" testifies to Canetti's admiration for Kafka; without replicating either the structure or the details it re-creates the nature of the Court against which K. vainly strives, especially in the third chapter of *The Trial*.)

Part 2 is concluded by Fischerle's murder. This part seems to lack the homogeneity of Part 1, and is in fact more episodic than integrated. As Canetti appears to indulge a less than ideally disciplined expansiveness, the action in Part 2 loses the concentrated focus that typified Part 1. The wonder may be that the young and inexperienced novelist manages to keep at least something of a steering-hold on his story.

Part 3, "The World in the Head," consists of but six chapters. It proceeds to the final cathartic incineration of Kien's library and his person—both of which are cathartic for the reader as well. The title reminds us that Kien's head is now full of infectious worldly misery *and* the books—a disparate and insupportable burden perhaps even for a sane person, certainly so for a madman.

Part 3 reflects the continuation of Canetti's loss of narrative control, the early signs of which were evident in Part 2. What had been a closed form in Part 1 is by now broken. The effect is that of fragmentation: full stories about characters only briefly mentioned heretofore, as of the psychiatrist

George Kien or the concierge Benedikt Pfaff; a frequently unmotivated accumulation of material that is not strictly relevant to the narration, or is relevant only tenuously, such as Canetti's theoretical and doctrinaire interpolations about crowds or madmen.

We should perhaps think of the theoretical interpolations as providing a retarding moment, in creating suspense before the cathartic denouement. But a larger part of the retarding moment may be related to the change in narrative viewpoint. Peter Kien is relegated to the wings while the narrative focuses on the life story of George Kien, with ample nonnarrative and theoretical interpolation. Such interpolation is a hallmark of the German novel compared with the American novel; one admires the skillful way in which Thomas Mann integrates the narrative with the critical or theoretical or philosophical. Canetti integrates much less persuasively—after all, *Auto-da-Fé* is a first novel. Similarly, late-in-the-novel change in narrative point of view, though supposedly a critical taboo, is not necessarily bad; in the hands of a skilled novelist like Arthur Schnitzler it can even add ironic depth. In the hands of the twenty-five or twenty-six-year-old Canetti it is a flaw, although far from a fatal one.

Canetti's chapter titles form an interesting commentary on the content of the given chapter. They also reveal his concern to control the epic breadth. The subtitling was thus a matter of some importance to him. He could, after all, have just used numbers without titles or have confined himself to objective titular summarizing. In fact he does use the latter method sometimes. The first chapter, "The Morning Walk," objectively summarizes what Peter Kien is doing at the outset. But many of the chapter titles are more imaginative or suggestive. Consider the final chapter. Describing the inferno of Kien's burning library, it is entitled "The Red Cock"—a German metaphor for fire (the translator—and implicitly Canetti, who supervised the translation—assume a considerable knowledge of German by the reader of the English translation). Sometimes a chapter title is simply a suggestive key-word, as in the second chapter of Part 3, "Trousers," which plays on the opposition of trousers and skirts—inspired by Benedikt Pfaff's peephole at the entry to the apartment complex. On this opposition is hung, by way of Krumbholz's leitmotivic blue skirt, a series of misogynistic aphorisms that perhaps passed as amusing in the 1930s; for example: "Women are illiterates, unendurable and stupid, a perpetual disturbance" (387).

Canetti achieves irony in entitling the life story of the monstrous Pfaff "The Kind Father," which is the first chapter in Part 3. (Actually in German it is "The Good Father," which has a more authentically ironic ring.)

Finally, the variety of Canetti's subtitling includes enigma. We have seen enigma already in the titles of the three parts, "A Head without a World," "Headless World," and "The World in the Head." In similar vein are certain chapter titles; for instance, that of the second chapter of Part 1, "The Secret." Krumbholz, newly employed by Kien, is obsessed by curiosity about what he is up to each morning between six-fifteen and seven. It is not research or writing. It must be drugs, she speculates. Then one morning she discovers that he ritualistically selects books for his briefcase and his morning walk. That secret is out, but we will not be disappointed if we expect that there will be more—whether or not relating to Kien.

The change of the narrative point of view from Peter Kien to George Kien occurs in the third chapter of Part 3, entitled descriptively and suggestively "A Madhouse," that is, the psychiatric hospital in Paris to whose directorship George has risen. The narrative focus returns to Peter Kien only with the final chapter, the metaphorically titled "The Red Cock." But the switch to George is only the solidest, lengthiest indication of a considerable narrational flexibility that in general, and with many an exception, proceeds from conventionally distanced third-person narration to an ever-closer identification of the author with his fictional characters. It is probably not by chance that this progression parallels the previously mentioned slackening of narrative pace as the novel proceeds. In a word, the characters take over.

Canetti's narrative method, as implied in the above, is varied and eclectic. At his best, and when he wants to, he successfully replicates the method of his idol, Kafka, by abandoning his intermediary role and placing the reader directly vis-à-vis the narrative situation. But Canetti may also station himself at some distance from the narrative and take ironic advantage of that distance. His technical methods—the use of dialogue, for example—are not revolutionary by present standards, but in the mid-1930s they represented a talented blending of those of the nineteenth century with the more daring and effective innovations developed by Kafka and Schnitzler. He can be, and often is, the third-person narrator who knows not only what is going on physically but also what is going on inside, let us say, Peter Kien's head.

At the other pole from omniscience he may, like a playwright, offer only the spoken words of a character or characters. The prime example of this technique is the opening dialogue between Peter Kien and Franz Metzger. The author tells us nothing; everything depends on what Kien and Metzger say to each other. This is also true in the dialogue between Kien and

Krumbholz in the ironically titled "The Million"—the one million schillings that Krumbholz, now Mrs. Kien, thinks Kien is withholding from her proper legacy.

Interior monologue is Canetti's fourth principal narrative method. There is no punctuation, such as quotation marks, to identify it. A nice example occurs in the also ironically titled chapter "Young Love," in Part 1. As Kien, supposedly suddenly enlightened about Krumbholz's love for him, flees the flat, memories of his wedding night flood his mind: "She lay down on the divan only for love of him. Women are sensitive to the mood of their beloved. She had understood his embarrassment" (121). And so on, Kien telling himself what had happened between them, his monologue conditioned by his recent enlightenment, which is no enlightenment.

It is difficult to specify with certainty just what the theme of *Auto-da-Fé* is, although that hasn't dissuaded critics from trying. It has been suggested that the book is a tribute to proud intellectuality in the lonely person of Peter Kien, coping with the crowd, buffeted by the cruel waves of twentieth-century philistinism and endemic violence. That suggestion has a comfortable, even cliché attractiveness to it—until we come up against the troublesome fact that Canetti is less than sympathetic with Kien as the latter confronts—reacts to, would be better—the travails placed in his way. He is mocked by all; he is subjected to devastating authorial irony. It is even possible to suggest the opposite: that *Auto-da-Fé* is a satire on the bookworm who makes his books his all and fails to have much interest in people.

The novel does contain an inordinate amount of violence—a parade of beatings and murders and sexual violence. Does that violence, taken together with the immolation of Kien and his books, make it prescient as to impending conditions and events under fascism? Not a small critical chorus asserts that is does, but such presumed prescience, when it is proved by hindsight, is suspect. By a comparable suspect token, Canetti's penchant for fictional violence and sadism could be said to be an early predictor of (especially American) television and films and the violence that is at home there and in society. It is a violent century; to that extent, Canetti *was* onto something.

Marxist interpretations of *Auto-da-Fé* are not lacking, although with the dissolution of Marxist political structures they are unlikely to become much more numerous. It seems hard to envision the novel as an allegorical invitation to Marxism to clean out the bourgeois stables, now that the Marxist stables have themselves been found other than sweet-smelling. In any event,

Canetti is no Marxist, even if as a budding artist he hobnobbed with Marxists and translated Upton Sinclair.

Yet Canetti is hardly an admirer of the bourgeoisie and their governments. And we still have to add in his admiration of Kafka, whom he understands better than most. If we take that with the seriousness it deserves, are we entitled to say that as with Kafka's people and things, the people and things in *Auto-da-Fé* don't stand for somebody or something else, that Canetti is aiming at a direct and absolute meaning? That interpretation too deserves consideration.

## NOTES

1. Alfons-M. Bischoff, *Elias Canetti: Stationen zum Werk* (Bern: Herbert Lang; Frankfurt am Main: Peter Lang, 1973) 37.
2. Angeles Cardona Castro, "Estudio especial del mundo novelesco de 'Die Blendung' de Elias Canetti," Roberto Corcoll and Marisa Siguán, eds. *Homenaje a Elias Canetti* (Kassel: Reichenberger, 1987) 75-139, esp. 98-99.
3. Elias Canetti, *Auto-da-Fé*, trans. C. V. Wedgwood (New York: Stein and Day, 1947) 120. Subsequent references are noted parenthetically.

# CHAPTER FOUR

# The Plays:
## *The Wedding; Comedy of Vanity; The Numbered*

Canetti's plays are probably the least-known part of his oeuvre. Ironically so, for he considers himself above all a dramatist. Why his plays are not well known is debatable; the following factors may all be relevant. There are only three—far too few to sustain a reputation as a playwright. They are "difficult" plays, intellectual satires likely to be inaccessible—or anathema—to many a playgoer and wholly unsuited to the Austrian Burgtheater tradition of realistic acting. From a dramatic point of view they are diffuse. Finally, the first two were written in the early 1930s, simultaneously with the rise of Nazism—an unlikely sponsor of unconventional dramas directed against the philistinism embodied by Nazism. These first two plays, *Hochzeit* (1932; *The Wedding*, 1986) and *Komödie der Eitelkeit* (written 1933–34; published 1950; *Comedy of Vanity*, 1934), had to wait a long time for their German premieres.

It will be useful here to examine Canetti's concept of the "acoustic mask," which finds its most concentrated employment in these early plays. It was in the 1920s that Canetti developed an ear for the voices of the city, for the outcries and the interjections. At the same time he noticed that people don't really talk *to* each other but rather *past* each other. People do not really understand each other, and in frustration they talk in ways that guarantee even more misunderstanding. What emerges linguistically from such a mode of (mis)understanding is the acoustic mask, the typical lexical-phonological fund of an individual speaker. The speaker has at his disposal some five hundred words, and he articulates them in a unique pattern of sequences and with a unique pattern of pitch, rhythm, and stress, of drawling and apocopating. Such an acoustic mask is as unique as a fingerprint and even harder to alter. It marks the speaker as different from every other speaker, even of the same language, even of the same dialect or jargon. It is uniquely *his;* it distinguishes him from every other speaker.

Canetti's acoustic mask, the theory of which he articulated in a 1937 interview in the Vienna newspaper *Der Sonntag*, to a large degree accords with what later linguistic theorists called the idiolect; that is, each speaker's private dialect, unlike that of any other speaker. Modern technology has largely confirmed what Canetti deduced from hearing and intuition. An idiolect, however—and probably an acoustic mask as well—is not necessarily confined to the simple and unreflective speaker. Indeed, Peter Kien in *Auto-da-Fé* had his, just as surely as did Therese Krumbholz—only it does not strike the reader as sharply as do Therese's subliterate utterances and impoverished vocabulary.

In its anticipation of linguistic theory, the acoustic mask is revealed as an essentially intellectual construct. That is, in its pure form it is an articulated sound, deficient in—or lacking completely—both ideology and dramatic meaning. Intellectualism or the constructs of intellectualism are subject to buffering and distancing in a novel such as *Auto-da-Fé*, and thus tolerable. For example, Krumbholz's recurring "Excuse me" and the like bear no dramatic weight; her "Excuse me" is simply another attribute of her character. In a work such as *Crowds and Power*, a creation of intellect rather than imagination, the acoustic mask can be quite at home. By the same token it amounts to a weakness in drama—a fish out of water, or rather an intellectualized fish in a dramatic sea, where it lacks the strength to sustain drama and move it forward.

As to the five hundred words that are declared by Canetti to comprise the everyday vocabulary of a speaker, and are thus an important component of his acoustic mask: In the first place, while his estimate may have been accurate for Germany or Austria in the 1920s, it might well be on the high side for the United States in the 1990s. Canetti wasn't suggesting a figure valid for all places at all times; we need only to guard against imagining five hundred to be after all no considerable vocabulary. In the second place, not being a linguist, Canetti seems to have made no provision for the fact that we all share a large percentage of our words with every other speaker of the same language. Only as the curve flattens does individuality manifest itself. In his favor, five hundred words naturally give greater opportunity for individual variation than do, say, 250. In any case he evidently finds the sound of language more important than vocabulary as an individual marker: he speaks of acoustic mask, not lexical mask.

In his emphasis on the acoustic aspect of language—how it impinges on the hearer's ear so as to comprise a unique marker—Canetti the author, the writer of words, has placed himself at the mercy of paradox. For to find readers he or any writer must write in a recognizable standard language—in his case German, although he ventures in *The Wedding* into not too recondite Viennese dialect. The point is, he cannot write in an international phonetic alphabet that reflects the actual individual phonological permutations that constitute the acoustic mask. What we get in its stead in *Auto-da-Fé* and in the two early plays is mostly an impoverished but characteristic lexical indicator that can *suggest* the acoustic mask. By the time the German is—even expertly—translated into English, the whole concept of the acoustic mask, not to say the lexical signal thereof, is apt to be much attenuated. That is, we sooner or later realize that Therese frequently says "Excuse me" when she takes exception to a statement by Kien or somebody else. That poverty-stricken interjection, so typical of her, and other such typical locutions have to *stand for* a much fuller linguistic portrait of Therese, one that distinguishes her sharply from every other character. It is a truism that those who would read Canetti have to work. In this light, whoever would savor his acoustic masks, Anglicized, has to exert imagination.

## The Wedding

The characters in *The Wedding* are recognizably demarcated by their acoustic masks. The parrot that repeatedly squawks on cue, "House. House. House," merely possesses the most concise mask, as well as the most significant thematically: the play revolves around the struggle to inherit a house from a grandmother who refuses to die, and the earthquake-caused collapse of the house, taking with it the crass partygoers attending the wedding of one Christa Segenreich. (Her last name, coined in obvious irony, means "rich in blessings.")

*The Wedding* opens with a prelude consisting of five short scenes. Each scene concisely demonstrates the poverty of the human relationships that revolve about the house. As is Canetti's habit of dramatic construction, there is no plot, no dramatic action in the usual sense. Functionally the prelude takes the place of the early exposition in typical plays, but when we get to the body of *The Wedding* the exposition does not give way to action. Only at the end is there action: the earthquake that destroys the house and its financially and sexually avaricious occupants.

The first scene has Grandmother Gilz, owner of the house, fighting off the greedy pressure and the indefatigable loquaciousness of her granddaughter Toni, who wants the house, and the sooner the better. Fortunately the old woman is deaf, in every sense, to Toni's pressure. As the parrot loudly takes up the cry of "House. House. House," both women are shouting at each other, Toni in the bargain threatening to strangle the bird. We may well suspect that as in *Auto-da-Fé* we are opening the door on life, or lives, in hell.

The second scene consists of a hardly more edifying discussion between an unspeakably pedantic high school teacher—Canetti's dramatic characters tend to be more caricature than character—and his wife, tenants in Mrs. Gilz's building. The teacher has the notion of heading off the importunities of Gilz's granddaughter by proposing to the old woman a lifelong annuity agreement by which, in return for guaranteed rent for as long as she lives, she will yield title to the building to the infant son of the teacher. To cap this infamous scheme the teacher will guarantee to assume responsibility for the parrot after Gilz's death. The only problem is, as his wife reminds him in a fishwifelike tirade, he lacks the courage to broach his scheme to the elderly would-be victim.

Scene 3 presents Peter, a thoroughly lovesick young man, and the object of his affections, the presumably chaste, pure, and clean Anita. There are indications that, with Peter at least, her chastity has been compromised. Be that as it may, she's going to the wedding party upstairs, won't be back before four in the morning; there's not much point—she strongly suggests—in Peter's waiting around that long. The exposition is moving along: we now know about the party. Probably not a party—to look ahead—that a chaste young lady would be going to.

The fourth scene of the prelude reveals a bit more about the house and its denizens. It is a dialogue between Gretchen, a businesswoman and investor, and her friend and business partner Max, a twenty-year resident of the building. Having talked with Mrs. Gilz about buying the building, he thinks he may have a deal, using Gretchen's money at five percent interest. He calls Gretchen ruthless; she accuses him of a lack of initiative because he isn't properly putting the squeeze on Gilz. He ought to inquire of the janitor about Gilz's health. But, says Max, the janitor is himself dying. No, corrects Gretchen, it's the janitor's wife who is dying. Max fears to press too much, but Gretchen will make him forget his fear. When Max tells her to take off her clothes, she shouts "Hallelujah."

The fifth scene presents the janitor and his dying wife, together with their ever-laughing, thirty-year-old daughter, a moron. Dance music from the floor above is already becoming louder—which bothers only slightly the janitor's reading aloud from his Bible. Nor does he heed his dying wife's pleas for attention. He is reading Judges 16:21ff., in which the Philistines take Samson and put out his eyes: "And he [Samson] said: Let me die with the Philistines. And he bowed himself with all his might; and the house fell upon the lords, and upon all the people that were therein''(v. 30). By now there can't be much doubt about who is partying in the house—''Philistines''—nor as to what is going to happen to them and the house: ''the house fell.'' That the partygoers are all killed in the crash is certified by the end of verse 30.

The body of the play is the wedding reception itself. Most of the characters in the prelude reappear, expressing themselves in ways that contradict what they have said in the prelude. They are joined by other partygoers and by the wedding principals: Christa, the bride, already making arrangements with three new admirers; her drunken father Herr Segenreich; her nymphomaniac mother Joanna; her brother Karl, a college sophomore and already an intellectual snob; and her fourteen-year-old sister Mary (Mariechen), apparently not a virgin Mary, for she can hardly make up her mind what male guest she should hop into bed with first. The bridegroom is Michael, who copulates with his new mother-in-law, Joanna.

There are numerous possibilities for Little Mary, including the bridegroom Michael. But the most spectacular would doubtless be the eighty-year-old Dr. Bock (= billy goat, stud). This pedophile has already ''treated'' the bride when she was twelve, not to mention her mother. On this occasion Dr. Bock is propositioning Pepi, the moronic daughter of the janitor and his moribund wife. While erotomania reigns, however, Christa is not unmindful of the dying wife of the janitor. Not only does Christa proclaim herself a better partner than Pepi, but the juxtaposition (or superimposition) of wedding party upstairs and putative corpse downstairs she finds hilarious.

Such are the modern (1930) Philistines as presented by playwright Canetti; such are the petty bourgeois who have ''made it,'' at least financially. What they aim for is material possession and sexual possession, and they are as crude in the pursuit of the one as of the other. It appears that Canetti's projected ''Human Comedy of Madmen'' that found partial expression in *Auto-da-Fé* finds dramatic continuation in *The Wedding*. The occasion of a wedding, marking the beginning of a new human relationship, serves as an ironically contrapuntal background to the spectacle of the disintegration, the corruption, the perversion of human relationships, for which the petty bourgeoisie on the make, in every sense, provides the ideal venue. The collapse of the building merely summarizes the variety of human collapse everywhere present during the wedding reception. While one may be too easily tempted to complain that the earthquake, so accurately foretold by the janitor's Bible reading, is a sort of deus ex machina, the matter is not that simple, since the fall of the building is a summary replication of the fall of its denizens.

At the height of the orgy the idealist Horch (whose name means "listen" or "hark") suggests a new party game. Supposing, he says, that in the midst of our party a bolt of lightning should come through the roof; no, make it an earthquake that causes this street to disappear into a hole, into which the building, with its residents and partygoers, tumbles. In fourteen minutes the end of the world. You may think it is a heavy truck at first, but it is a cataclysmic temblor. What, at this telling moment, will you do for the person you love the most?

Each guest is called upon to name the person dearest to him or her and to describe what steps he will take to rescue that person when he hears the truck that is not a truck. The guests, however, thinking it only another inconsequential party game, merely lie to each other (as Horch, the realistic idealist, knows they will). That is, since all of their interpersonal relationships are lies anyway—based on lust and greed—they continue to lie to each other. What each does for his or her dearest when the quake actually strikes is—nothing. As the building goes down, each is concerned only to save his own skin. In the groans following the collapse, the voice of the janitor's dying but still alive wife is heard. Then that of Grandmother Gilz. Finally that of the parrot: "House. House. House!"

Although *The Wedding* was Canetti's first-written and first-published drama, its German premiere took place nine months after that of *Comedy of Vanity*. *The Wedding* was first presented on 3 November 1965 at the State Theater in Brunswick. It lasted for just seven performances, but that was long enough to unleash an earthquake of moral outrage, duly recorded and commented on in the press and on the radio. Canetti's name and reputation were attacked with such concerted venom—he was accused of obscenity— that a kind of artistic rescue operation was mounted by his confederates in the literary and critical world. It remained for Theodor W. Adorno to accurately locate *The Wedding* as a conflation of German expressionism of the World War I years with the then contemporary theater of the absurd. In Adorno's words the play represents "a literary-historic compromise between German expressionism, already faded from the stage, and the contemporary so-called theater of the absurd." With, it should be added, an admixture of Romanticism in its recourse to play within a play (Horch's what-would-you-do-if game), as well as, much more faintly, Viennese satire in the tradition of Karl Kraus and Ödön von Horváth. Something like what was to become Canetti's acoustic mask may seem to be discernible in the limited, cliché-ridden language of Horváth's lower-middle-class characters. But the latter are characters with whom we engage, not the rather cardboard types who inhabit Canetti's acoustic masks.

## Comedy of Vanity

The shadow of Karl Kraus may with effort be seen in the scenes comprising *Comedy of Vanity*, but while the persiflage of Kraus's characters in *The Last Days of Mankind* is invariably true to life, Canetti's characters are, again, largely caricatures and in no case convincingly real. The theme, on the other hand, is actual: the necessity of vanity to the human condition, the persistence, the pervasiveness of vanity that thrives even in the extirpation of vanity.

In the first part of the play—which consists of three parts, each containing a succession of scenes—the government, evidently a dictatorship, has issued a proclamation forbidding the possession and use of mirrors as well as the future manufacture thereof. Existing mirrors must be destroyed. After a thirty-day grace period possession or use of a mirror will be punished with a prison sentence of twelve to twenty years. The manufacture of mirrors is punishable by death. What is said of mirrors applies also to photographs of humans or humanlike creatures, or to any other form of human likeness.

This law seems not to have been sanctioned by any legislative body but to be simply an edict issued by the government. Herein lies a readily observable paradox, an irony. Imagine the vanity of a government that, to eliminate vanity in its subjects, is prepared to enforce such draconian measures! The effect is mass hysteria among the populace, complete disorientation—no wonder, when we take into consideration the fundamentality of the mirror, beginning in early childhood, to the individual's concept of self. But on the other hand the smashing of mirrors and the burning of pictures offer an initial exercise in the exertion of power by the oppressed and the inadequate—for example, the otherwise stuttering teacher, Schackerl, who declaims fluently when reading the government pronouncement, or the packer with a bale of pictures to be consigned to the fire, who threatens to destroy the entire city.

In short, the governmental proclamation has bred not only mass disorientation but also fanaticism. In a play written in 1933–34 the proscription, the burning and smashing, the fanaticism, the loss of humanity reflect all too precisely what was actually going on in contemporary Nazi Germany shortly after Hitler's rise to power. Hitler conscripted youth into the ranks of supporters if not perpetrators of government-endorsed arson and thuggery. Canetti presents one Kaldaun, Junior, still in a baby carriage, screamingly exhorting, "Fire! Fire!" And, tellingly, a decent, worn-out worker is named Franzl Nada—the last name meaning "nothing" in Spanish.

The second part of *Comedy of Vanity* takes place ten years later: life without mirrors or pictures. In spite of the outlawing of these reflectors of the human image, vanity has not been eliminated. Some people obey the law; others contrive in various ways to circumvent it. There is a lively black market in mirror fragments. And sycophancy becomes a service industry. Nada, an erstwhile public porter, makes an art of verbose flattery of passersby. If he also makes a decent income in the process, his name has become more appropriate than ever: income up, self-esteem at zero.

The regime is equally resourceful. It issues a decree whereby anglers are required to turn their backs when fishing so as not to see themselves reflected in the water before them. Puddles of rainwater achieve importance for their reflective qualities. While all this evokes a sense of absurdity, it is on the whole not more absurd than reality in Germany in 1933 and 1934. (Austria was not far behind in its Austrofascist coup of 1934.) The system works in such a way that everyone comes to distrust everyone else, for the regime has its spies and denouncers in every quarter. This, however, does not prevent even the noisiest advocates of the regime, driven like everyone else by the threat of depersonalization, from illegally trying to catch a glimpse of themselves.

Part 3 takes us to an illegal—but by both sexes exceedingly well-patronized—business established to satisfy that inherent drive: the cold-eyed but smiling Emilie Fant's grandiose hall of mirrors. For a handsome admission fee one is provided with seated access to a mirror, before which one postures and, in the excess of excitement, abstains from breathing. No one knows who his neighbor at the next seat is, and would be frightened if he did; but self-absorption guarantees as much as walls could. In fact, though, in a superprice range, there are luxury private cabins.

The play's resolution—as in *The Wedding* seemingly arbitrary but in fact integral—is induced by Heinrich Föhn, a regular at Mrs. Fant's hall of mirrors. With a recording supplying the ovations at the touch of a button, Föhn in his luxury cabin stands in view of his mirror image and delivers a speech resonant with the phony phrases associated with fascism—a word not actually used in the play. Each of Föhn's spurious slogans touches a different customer in the salon of mirrors. Revolt gathers and erupts.

Every customer, grabbing a mirror in egoistic revalidation, shouts, "I! I! I! I! I! I! I! I! I! I! I! I! I! I!" The crowd presses out onto the street, everyone holding up a mirror or a picture of himself and shouting, "I! I! I! I! I! I!" It is indeed a revolt but hardly a noble one, suffused as it is with the Canettian feeling that to survive, to feed his ego, each person will do what he has to do.

*Comedy of Vanity* premiered at the State Theater of Brunswick on 6 February 1965—more than thirty years after it was written (and twenty after the military defeat of the regime it apparently satirizes). Eight performances were given. There was no scandal; instead unanimous critical disapproval centered on the staging and direction. For example, isn't it amply clear what the play is about without cluttering up the stage with pictures of Hitler? But inevitably criticism of the production was transmuted into criticism of the playwright. The general rumble of disapprobation probably paved the way for the scandal that attended the production of *The Wedding* nine months later in the same playhouse by the same company. *Comedy of Vanity* had a different, very successful production in Basel in 1978.

## The Numbered

Canetti's third, much later play, is *Die Befristeten* (1952). English translations bear two different titles. That by Gitta Honegger is called *Life-Terms* (1982); that by Carol Stewart, *The Numbered* (1984). *Die Befristeten* are people who have had a time limit placed on their lives. In Canetti's play it is an arbitrary limit—you will live so many years—and it is imposed at birth by a government functionary. For that reason—and above all because of the political and social control that flows from such a limitation—the regime and the society in question are sometimes called totalitarian by critics. Perhaps, but again—and even more so than in *Comedy of Vanity*—we are not dealing with a *drame à clef*. Calling *The Numbered* totalitarian seems to miss the point, the theme of it all. The play takes place in an anti-Utopia set up to come to grips with death's encroachment on socially productive life. The effort fails, for reasons shortly to become evident.

*The Numbered* represents a melding of Canetti's concern with crowds, power, and survivorship (as in *Crowds and Power*) and his equally long-standing concern with death. Representing as it does a variety—and perhaps not a dramatically integrable variety—of Canetti's concerns, *The Numbered* suffers from the absence of a clear ideological focus. Which is it: a play about power and survival or a play about transformation and vanquishing death? That Canetti connects these themes theoretically does not guarantee their viability all together in a drama, whose ideological expansibility is limited.

Like its predecessor plays, *The Numbered* ends in collapse and calamity, even, if the party in *The Wedding* is a form of rebellion, in rebellion, collapse, and calamity. It is highly schematic, quite abstract, a long way from Aristotelian drama and almost as far from that of Brecht. Still, it is a well-wrought play as far as dialogue is concerned, and not coincidentally it depends less on the acoustic mask.

The first part opens with a mother chasing after her little boy. The boy is named Seventy. That is his foreordained life span; he doesn't have to worry about dying until his seventieth birthday. His mother, on the other hand, is destined to die at thirty-two, not far off, a hundred-and-some goodnight kisses. In successive scenes we discover that each person's birth date and death date are contained in a locket worn about the neck, sealed by the functionary Keeper at birth, opened by the Keeper at death. Those dates are supposed to be known only to the wearer of the locket.

What happens, though, is that people with names like Seventy are esteemed, for they are sure to be around awhile. Guessing age from appearance, one can afford to make an emotional investment in such people. Guessing ages is one of the malicious social by-products of a system designed to foster regularized contentment and immunity from competition and violence. People with names from Forty on down are not in much social demand. If no one can die, either naturally or by violence, before his "moment," then murder ceases to be a possibility. And while guessing another's age is common, telling one's own age is a crime.

With one exception everyone is attuned to the system that proscribes self-revelation, makes murder passé, substitutes certainty for doubt and tranquillity for ferment. The single outsider to the system and rebel against it is Fifty, who is presented in the second scene in a dialogue with his Friend. Fifty's skepticism is coming alive. Or perhaps it is already fully formed but is revealed to us only in increments. In any case it eventually takes the form of smashing his own locket to confirm his suspicion that all the lockets are a fraud—containing nothing.

With Fifty's breach of the taboo, the whole house of cards built on the taboo comes tumbling down. People are exhilarated by their newly found freedom, by the abandonment of the rigid and disagreeable social norms that had been imposed by the now collapsed system. But wait! Fear, formerly reserved for a single, predictable, life-terminating moment, is now back to bedevil man throughout his life. Aggression, unhindered by repression, is back, murder too. Fifty comes to regret his destruction of the taboo. People cannot bear the revelation that the taboo was a fake. But as chaos reigns, it is too late to undo the undoing.

*The Numbered* premiered in English at the Playhouse Theatre, Oxford, on 5 November 1956. The German original, *Die Befristeten,* received its premiere on 11 November 1967 at the Kleines Theater in der Josefstadt, Vienna. Playing for five weeks, it was accorded unanimous critical approval.

Despite varying critical reception ranging from scandal to a high degree of approval, Canetti's plays, taken as a whole, seem unlikely to become more than occasionally produced vehicles of more literary and historic than dramatic interest. They lack dramatic development and urgency, the conflict of protagonist and antagonist. It is almost traditional to berate nondramatic drama for intellectuality and abstractness, yet precisely those qualities strike us as endemic to Canetti's plays, perhaps not quite so much in *The Wedding* as in the more distinctly philosophical *Comedy of Vanity* and *The Numbered*. One rarely is compelled to engage with a character, and then not for long. The character's acoustic mask is always of interest, yet it does not necessarily contribute to a dramatic character.

# CHAPTER FIVE

# Crowds and Power

Canetti's masterwork as a thinker is the nonfictional *Masse und Macht* (1960; *Crowds and Power*, 1962). The work was begun in the early 1930s, and there followed a long but not continual period of writing and rewriting beginning in 1948. *Crowds and Power* receives surprisingly skimpy attention from literary critics, possibly because they imagine it to be beyond their purview. In fact it is useful in establishing the bases and development of Canetti's thinking as reflected in his fiction, his dramas, and his essays. It is especially relevant to *Auto-da-Fé*; around 1930 Canetti was working both on the novel and with the materials for *Crowds and Power*.

Canetti's rejection of Freudian theory is marked throughout his writing. The figure of George Kien, the psychiatrist brother of Peter, is to a striking degree—though the fit is not perfect—a send-up of Freudian psychiatry, some methods of which—for example, hypnosis—originally had Parisian roots. *Masse und Macht* (the alliterative German title is literally translated "Mass and Might") was born of Canetti's negative assessment of Freud's *Group Psychology and the Analysis of the Ego*. Freud's title reveals his point of view: the crowd as a threat to the ego of the individual. Canetti, on the contrary, wants to work from the point of view of the crowd: what causes a crowd to be born, what makes it grow, what causes it to dissolve.

Canetti's method reflects but little of his academic training as a chemist, a scientist. Instead of single-mindedly directing his efforts toward the original condition or documentation of a phenomenon, as Freud did, Canetti was tireless in his quest for a breadth of documentation, which he marshals but does not categorize. This does not preclude a respectable list of original sources, but there is a lack of conceptual system and step-by-step development. The result is a dazzling panoply of data, much of which, however, would be subject to the charge of being anecdotal.

When one rereads, however, an underlying linear development seems to emerge, not without a disconcerting amount of stopping and starting—and even zigzagging—as Canetti follows his fancy as much as he does a straight line. In general the direction is from crowds to the concept of power, from power to the closely related notion of the survivor (the wielder of effective power), and back to a much more detailed discussion of power. Here the survivor, having been introduced, is kept in the wings, as it were, to reemerge—"mankind's worst evil"[1]—as the final topic.

The broad categories above are Canetti's. But on the whole, and increasingly as detail increases, he deeply mistrusts categories and categorization—here one sees another nucleus of his disaffection with Freud—and as he much later explains, he was at pains to avoid anything resembling a conceptual system. Small wonder that *Crowds and Power,* called poetic, or rather poetic anthropology, by humanists,[2] wasn't called anything at all by scientists; it appears to lack any reception in those quarters.

What Canetti derives from his array of anthropological, psychological, sociological, philosophical, historical, and political data—predominantly the first two—is a study of the types of crowds, the development of crowds, and the state of mind of crowds; in other words, a typology derived from ostensive noncategorization. And several external events seem to have been involved. The assassination of the German prime minister Walter Rathenau in 1922, the torching of the Vienna Palace of Justice and the consequent police murders in 1927, the brief civil war in Austria in 1934 that resulted in the dominance of Austrofascism impelled Canetti's research and writing (and rewriting) in the direction not only of a general typology of crowd phenomena but also of a typology of the root causes of fascism.

A book as diverse and extensive (555 pages in the German soft-bound edition, 495 pages in its American counterpart) is not well suited to conclusive summarizing. For that reason our discussion will follow approximately the linear development of its thought. Some parts of the work, usually lengthy exemplifications, are heavily anecdotal. Yet these engaged Canetti's interest and ought not to be entirely omitted in a balanced consideration of what he was up to with *Crowds and Power.* As always in his writings—and more so than usual—he envisions an erudite, certainly a perceptive and critical, readership.

Like *Auto-da-Fé, Crowds and Power* is divided at the first level into several parts or sections, each part containing in turn a number of titled chapters. By reading the four- or five-page table of contents one can glean an overview of the direction of the book. The text of *Crowds and Power* is divided into twelve sections. The number of chapters in each section ranges from twenty-four (in the first section, "The Crowd") to one (in the epilogue). There is accordingly a sense of gradual refinement and distillation, even though the number of chapters in the intervening sections would not produce a consistently descending graph line. But the sense of extensive ground-laying, of touching many bases, is unmistakable in the first section.

The chapter-titles are fundamentally descriptive; not a trace of irony. What suggestibility exists is owing to descriptive brevity. For example, "Rhythm" suggests by its very brevity, whereas "The Fear of Being Touched," the first chapter of all, is more explicit than suggestive (though not entirely lacking in the latter quality).

In this first short chapter—all the early chapters are just a page or two in length—Canetti notes that the touch of the unknown is man's deepest fear. We are familiar with the convention of maintaining a certain personal space around us, although the dimensions of the space may vary somewhat according to our culture or cultural origin. While this space derives from the innate fear of being touched, one is liberated—at first glance paradoxically—from this fear by being in a crowd, and the denser the crowd the better. For one stops fearing the touch of the crowd; all are equal in a crowd; there is protection—and not merely physical—in a crowd. So a crowd enlists members and takes on a dynamism of its own. As Canetti puts it in the second chapter, "The Open and the Closed Crowd," "the urge to grow is the first and supreme attribute of the crowd"(16).

The natural form of the crowd is what Canetti calls "the open crowd": open in that there are no limits placed on its growth; open also on every side and in every direction. Growth is essential to the open crowd; should it cease to grow, it will disintegrate. The closed crowd, in contrast, accepts a limitation on growth—whether physical, financial, or personal—as a guarantee of (relative) permanence. It assumes continuance effected by repeated dissolution and reassembly. The rapid change from a closed to an open crowd is called the eruption.

In the next chapter Canetti discusses what he denotes as "the most important occurrence within the crowd" (17). That is the "discharge"; from the German original we gather that the analogy is indeed electrical. It is the moment when members of a crowd shed—discharge—their differences and feel themselves to be equals. The discharge, the feeling of equality, is illusory, however; it may obfuscate but it cannot eradicate inherent difference. Absent new members and renewed discharge, the crowd will disintegrate.

Crowds tend to be destructive, or at least to attack all imposed boundaries, which produces destruction. Of the modes of destruction the most impressive is fire, owing both to its high visibility and its irrevocability. (It is useful to consider the preceding statement in conjunction with the spectacular fire set by the individual, Peter Kien, to incinerate himself and his library.) Fire or no, a crowd never gets its fill of destruction as long as a single person remains inaccessible to it.

"Domestication of Crowds in the World Religions" dwells on a variation of one of Canetti's prime antipathies, namely, the world's major religions. Having themselves grown suddenly and unexpectedly through crowd dynamics, well-established religions possess a keen sense of the treacherousness of crowds and contrive to set their goals in the distant future—paradise or heaven—to neutralize the crowd's tendency to grow quickly. Repetition —as of liturgy—is the agent of this neutralization.

In the chapter entitled "Panic" Canetti not surprisingly reverts to the subject of fire. The panicked individual fights to escape because the crowd, in a state of disintegration, is imperiled. The erstwhile crowd assumes the quality of fire. The fire becomes, is, a hostile crowd, and has become etched in the mind of man as a symbol of the crowd. This statement bears consideration in the case of Peter Kien. If the final fire is the symbol of the crowd—the "world," in the vocabulary of the novel—then it may be seen as one more, climactic, dimension of Kien's alienation from that world. The fire, the world, then consumes both Kien and his books. And, not to forget, it was set by Kien.

Possibly as a result of his early exposure to soccer crowds at the field near his rented quarters in Hacking, Canetti does not neglect to consider the crowd as a ring. He devotes a chapter to such a crowd, which is doubly closed. That is, both physically and emotionally it is closed to the world outside as well as to the world within itself. The number of seats is limited. Each spectator faces a thousand others, so that—quite apart from the excitement generated by the game—he is infected by their excitement and they by his. He implies the effect of stadium conformation by noting that the effect of a closed ring is that of precluding escape.

A summarizing chapter entitled "The Attributes of the Crowd" lists four important crowd traits: "1. The crowd always wants to grow. . . . 2. Within the crowd there is equality. . . . 3. The crowd loves density. . . . 4. The crowd needs a direction" (29). In the case of the fourth trait, direction is to be understood in the sense of goal. In addition to the open/ closed distinction there is a distinction between the stagnating crowd and the rhythmic crowd. The stagnating crowd desires a prolonged period of density before discharge—that is, equality—occurs, while in the rhythmic crowd (for example, in the dance) density and equality coincide from the start and are both embodied in movement. In a separate chapter on rhythm Canetti quotes at length from a description of the haka, originally a war dance of the New Zealand Maoris. This is the first of many such extended quotations that are incorporated into the text of *Crowds and Power.* His sources run the gamut from classic and well-known works—for example, Bernal Díaz del Castillo's *The Discovery and Conquest of Mexico*—to highly specialized and obscure treatises.

Crowds do not have to be seen dancing or sitting in a soccer stadium; they can be invisible. Canetti has a chapter on "Invisible Crowds," that is, crowds of the invisible dead. His survey of this kind of crowd ranges from Bechuanaland in South Africa to the Tlingit Indians of Alaska, but the instance familiar to most readers will be that of Valhalla of Norse (here called Germanic) mythology. Valhalla is the heaven of the numberless warriors who have fallen in battle and who now reap their reward in ever-renewable food and drink, as well as in more fighting.

According to their emotional content, Canetti distinguishes five types of crowds, devoting a chapter to explication and discussion of each: (1) baiting crowds, (2) flight crowds, (3) prohibition crowds, (4) reversal crowds, and (5) feast crowds. The baiting crowd is ancient, going back to man's early hunting packs. This horde can mete two kinds of death penalty: expulsion, such as putting the individual out at the mercy of wild animals or starvation; and collective killing, such as stoning the individual, consigning him to flames, or crucifying him. The victim is literally baited by the crowd, which disintegrates quickly after the slaying.

Although the term "flight crowd" has been rendered ambiguous by modern technology—it seems to conjure up a picture of a crowded airport—Canetti had in mind a crowd fleeing a threat. Such a mass flight toward real or imagined safety generates a substantial force, an impetus that can last for days or weeks. A flight crowd, coherent and tenacious, dissolves only upon the attainment of safety. Examples are the retreat of Napoleon's army from Moscow or the French evacuation of Paris upon the approach of the Germans in 1940.

A prohibition crowd is a crowd that comes together to refuse to do what the individual members have been doing singly. Because it centers on the act of refusal, it may be termed a negative crowd. The most pertinent example is a strike. At the moment a strike is called, the workers, from the highest to the lowest paid, become equals. Through organization the strike crowd carries out the functions of a state, a state with few, but inviolable laws: no strikebreaking by crowd members, no scabbing by would-be replacement workers, fair—that is, equal—distribution of limited resources. In this posture the negative crowd in peaceful and self-disciplined. If the strike falters, though, or if material want becomes unbearable, or in the case of violence against it, the negative crowd will revert to a positive crowd and engage in violence.

A reversal crowd is a revolutionary crowd. Its seedbed is a stratified society, one in which a higher group issues commands to a lower, less powerful group. "Every command," says Canetti in a statement more fundamental than its present applicability to reversal crowds, "leaves behind a painful *sting* in the person who is forced to carry it out" (58). Those aggrieved singly by sting can band together and turn on those who have been issuing commands. The discharge of such a crowd is chiefly in its deliverance from the sting of commands. The storming of the Bastille is typically thought to mark the beginning of the French Revolution. But, to use Canetti's metaphor, before the sheep dare attack the wolves, they turn on the hares. By this reckoning the Revolution began not on Bastille Day, July 14, but rather in June, and not in Paris but in Brittany, where some fifty young people—already a reversal crowd—destroyed four to five thousand hares while the game wardens looked on ineffectively. Another instance of a reversal crowd is the crowd that participates in religious "revivals." The crowd is terrified by the sting of the preacher until, in extreme cases, it collapses and lies as though dead. When it comes to, it is changed, it is "born again," for death or a semblance of death has preceded the rebirth. In the religious instance we can most clearly see Canetti's aetiology of the crowd as insistently unique. It is relatively persuasive, but one has the feeling—possibly conditioned by our Freudian era—that other factors, individual psychological factors, may well be in play in religious "revivals," factors that manifest themselves under the license of a crowd situation.

The feast crowd is just what the term implies. An abundance of good things—not only to eat—is the key. Further, a densely populated feast suggests continued increase of food and people, of life. The feast crowd is joyful and sanguine.

So much for crowds classified according to their dominant emotion. Now Canetti turns his attention to what he calls the double crowd. A second, related crowd may be essential to the existence or well-being of the first crowd. There may be tension between the two, perhaps owing to a ritual game, perhaps owing to the relationship itself; but in the face of a common, life-threatening enemy the two groups will unite. The full chapter title is suggestive: "The Double Crowd: Men and Women. The Living and the Dead." That men and women comprise a double crowd is everywhere manifest. The living and the dead also comprise a double crowd of which the two parts are continually interacting. The actions and reactions of the living are everywhere colored by the image of the much more numerous and more powerful crowd of the dead, those who have already crossed over and whom the living must sooner or later join. The fight—it is a fight—is a mismatch, and the living are always in retreat.

The third sort of double crowd, whose dissolution Canetti—and surely not only Canetti—would welcome, is that called into existence by war: military adversaries. Each side, in striving to prevail over—that is, to kill the larger proportion of—its enemy, is dependent on the other. The heap of dead is thought of as a unit: Canetti offers examples from Germanic and Anglo-Saxon antiquity, from the prophet Mohammed, from ancient Egypt and Assyria. The reluctance of an army to end a war, even though it may be a losing war, is owing to its desire to remain a crowd, not to disintegrate. If the crowd should disintegrate, the war must end, and with it the opportunity to forestall one's own death by slaying adversaries. In this latter contingency we see evidence of Canetti's sophisticated reasoning on a topic that engages him deeply on two fronts: his passionate commitment to the end of wars and warring, and his equally passionate commitment to survive the encroachments of death.

Next Canetti defines a term that he uses frequently in the remainder of *Crowds and Power:* crowd crystal. "Crowd crystals are the small, rigid groups of men . . . which serve to precipitate crowds" (73). Crowd crystals must be unified; their number must be constant; their overall purpose needs to be obvious, although individuals may be allotted distinctive roles in the overall purpose. They are nuclei; or possibly the Marxist term "cadres" conveys the idea most precisely (not that Canetti uses it, or any other Marxist terminology).

The last chapter of the first section, the longest chapter so far, is a kind of glossary of crowd symbols or metaphors often used for the crowd. They are only metaphors, we are reminded, they are only *"felt* to be a crowd" (75); but because they shed light on the crowd, a consideration of them can be profitable. The first crowd symbol is fire. Fire is always the same. Fire is contagious, insatiable, sudden. It can break out anywhere. It is multiple; consider, says Canetti, the plural forms "flames" and "tongues of flame." Fire is destructive. Fire has enemies; it seems to be alive and is treated as if it were. All of these attributes it shares with the crowd. Significantly, Canetti declares that the propensity to incendiarism is the most strikingly dangerous trait of the crowd. It is also the most life-threatening propensity of Peter Kien.

Incendiarism originated in the burning of forests (and is still widely practiced in slash-and-burn agriculture). Thus the origin of arson. Arson is a fixed idea; the arsonist feels compelled to it as if by an invisible force and loves to watch the resultant fire. Here Canetti, whose foremost experience of arson was no doubt as a witness to the burning of the Palace of Justice in 1927, comes tantalizingly close—but still doesn't take the final half-step—to the generally accepted post-Freudian interpretation, according to which the arsonist may indeed admire the fire, which, however, he has set to call attention to himself and to expose himself to the likelihood of apprehension.

The sea too is a powerful metaphor for the crowd, though less compelling than that of fire. The sea contains all life. The sea is multiple in its waves and drops. Like a crowd it moves, it has density, it is cohesive. It has a voice. The sea is changeable in its mood. It remains in existence forever, just as a crowd desires to do.

Rain, variable in its density, symbolizes the crowd at the moment of discharge as well as in the period of disintegration. Rivers are a persuasive crowd symbol—especially of a forming crowd—moving unremittingly in a given direction, absorbing other streams along the way. To be sure, a river's width is fixed; on the other hand it can overflow its banks.

The forest, taller than man, forms a protective arch over him. It compels man to glance upward in awe, as if he were in church. In its immobility and resistance the forest has also become the symbol of the crowd that is a tenacious army. Grain ("corn" in *Crowds and Power*) is a lesser, and less mighty, forest. It is pliant, unresisting, like a group of loyal subjects. In its image men see their equality in the face of death. And it signifies increase, whether in the field or heaped at harvest. Indeed the heap, whether of grain or other comestibles, is itself an important symbol for the crowd. One thinks of its denseness and its capacity to sustain. The stone heap calls to mind its innumerable builders.

The wind, gathering everything to itself, resembles a growing crowd. And invisible, it symbolizes the invisible crowd. Wind makes sand shift; wind-blown sand lies halfway between being a fluid and a solid symbol. Like a crowd sand is made up of many small units, apparently equal to each other, and boundless. Finally sand, as frequently instanced in the Bible, has become a symbol of progeny.

Canetti's final metaphor for the crowd is treasure, the accumulation of treasure—one might say the heaps of treasure. Greed unites people in their confidence in the components of the treasure, that is, in money. If the value of monetary treasure depreciates, the bearer of the devalued money likewise feels depreciated. Until—Canetti is clearly speaking from his experience of the catastrophic German inflation of 1923—they come together in groups that resemble flight crowds. The underlying principle is: "The more people lose, the more united are they in their fate" (90).

The second section of *Crowds and Power* is devoted to "The Pack." Both crowd crystals and crowds, Canetti declares, derive from the older unit, the pack, in which they are still undifferentiated. The pack cannot grow; there is no one who could join it. Or rather, as Canetti later amends, if the pack does grow, it is through a temporary alliance with another pack, an alliance that does not affect the retention of a separate consciousness. In the original conception of the static pack, pack members were intensely ambitious to be more numerous, to be less limited. Lacking numbers—such as would be supplied by an alliance—they were obliged to compensate by resorting to intensity.

We recall that the four essential attributes of the crowd are growth, density, equality, and direction. As far as the pack is concerned, the first two of these are fictitious, merely acted out. Equality and direction, however, do genuinely exist in the pack. They are in fact all the more intensely present owing to the absence of growth and density. Unswerving direction is the first thing one notices about the pack, while its equality is expressed in a common devotion to the same goal.

The pack exhibits four different forms, synonymous with different functions: the hunting pack; the war pack, closely related to the hunting pack; the lamenting pack; and the increase pack. Canetti devotes a chapter to each of the four forms. Common to all four is the ability of one form to transform into another. Such transmutation always has consequences, as in the development of strange myths and cults when a hunting pack changes into a lamenting pack and the lamenters want to obliterate the fact that they were once hunters.

The hunting pack moves over a large area to kill a living object that it wants to "incorporate," that is, eat. Movement is of the essence. Equally important is a peaceful distribution made according to well-established rules. The war pack differs essentially from the hunting pack in that the former is only half of a formation. That is, for a pack to be a true war pack there must be two groups—both composed of male warriors—facing off against each other. Canetti then illustrates and documents his concepts with extended quotations from a source not identified in the text.

To describe the lamenting pack Canetti turns to the Warramunga aborigines of Central Australia and their mode of lamenting the dying and the dead. Two factors emerge as fundamental to the development of a lamenting pack. After a violent movement toward the dying person an aroused throng—some of whose members have mutilated themselves—forms about him. Thereafter comes a terrified flight away from the dead man and from whatever he may have touched.

The increase pack is more complex than the packs described above. The typically obscured processes of increase need to be grasped in conjunction with the processes of transformation. Because the idea of transformation pervades Canetti's literary writing—in a sense it is the uniquely developed precipitate of his admiration of Kafka, and in the German text he uses and italicizes the Kafkan term *Verwandlung* (transformation or metamorphosis)—we will emphasize it appropriately here. For Canetti, transformation is fundamentally linked to the desire to be more. The member of the increase pack, wanting to be more, incorporates into himself the animals he knows, and this is done by transformation. Canetti's transformational scheme, however, does not imply a simple case of A *becoming* B, but of A incorporating B into himself and thereby becoming *more* than he was.

The ancestors celebrated in aboriginal myths—we hear of the Pueblo Indians and the Australian aborigines—are the products of transformation. The ancestors, having succeeded in looking and feeling like, say, a kangaroo, became transformed into a kangaroo—a kangaroo totem. When word of this transformation was handed down to succeeding generations, it became the stuff of myths. Myths are then the confirmation and avenue of transformation.

The link between increase and transformation is reflected in the frequency with which vermin—notoriously prolific—appear as totems, for instance, grubs, termites, grasshoppers, lice, flies, and mosquitoes. The immense population of such vermin makes them desirable for inclusion as totems. And similarly with clouds, rain, fire, wind, sand, the sea, and stars—all prominent totems of the Australian aborigines.

Communion, the topic of Canetti's next chapter, is the rite of incorporation by the group. The animal eaten at communion is treated deferentially; for then it will revive and allow itself to be hunted again. Then, as is always true, the hunting pack will change into an increase pack, and transformation will recur. In "higher" religions (what is meant by "higher" is left unexplained) another increase factor is allied with communion: the increase of the faithful as well as the increase in food. One thinks of the New Testament miracle by which a multitude of hungry people was fed with a few loaves of bread and a few fish.

The practice of communion marks a transition from an outward to an inward pack. An outward pack moves toward an external goal. An inward pack forms around a recently dead man who must be buried. By the vociferousness of the lament one may further distinguish between the noisy pack, strident while facing the enemy, and the tranquil pack, full of expectation, which it reinforces by chants, exorcisms, or sacrifices.

The last two chapters of the second section are devoted to the pack in the ancestor legends of the Aranda aborigines of Australia. But first Canetti directs our attention to the historic permanence of packs. Many archaic elements persisting in modern cultures—for example, fox-hunting in England—find their expression in a pack. One "unashamedly primitive pack" still survives—or did at the time when Canetti wrote—namely, the pack that operates under the name and warrant of lynch law. The sexual accusation that ritually precedes the invocation of lynch law has the effect of transforming the target of the mob into a dangerous being, something like a wild animal.

The third section of *Crowds and Power* is titled "The Pack and Religion." We recall that each form of pack, upon attaining its goal, tends to change into another form. Some such transformations have been taken out of the larger context and become fixed, reproduced identically over and over, as the substance of every important religion. Canetti goes so far as to assert that "the dynamics of packs . . . explains the rise of the world religions" (128). This aetiology is clearly far removed from that in Freud's *Moses and Monotheism,* although a detailed comparison might turn up some identity of detail.

There are religions of hunting, such as that practiced by the Lele tribe, who live near the Kasai River in Zaire. In spite of its skimpy rewards, the communal hunt is the focus of Lele social and religious life. There are religions of war, such as that of the Jivaros of southern Ecuador and northwestern Peru, who go to war to gain the booty of their enemies' heads, duly shrunken. (The Jivaros are hunters as well.) Both war and hunting have died out among the Pueblo Indians of the American Southwest, among whom the lamenting pack consequent on death has been all but suppressed. Rain and corn comprise the center of their religion, and they live, above all, for peaceful increase.

Canetti inserts two chapters dealing with the dynamics of war (the role of the first dead man in the starting of wars and "Islam as a Religion of War") to set the scene for his consideration of what he calls the religions of lament, which have spread over the world and—this seems an exaggeration—"unified it." Certainly it is true, though, as he phrases it some pages later, that the religions of lament have changed the face of the earth (128, 143). What, he asks rhetorically, has endowed them with their resiliency, their millennia-long persistence?

Such religions form around the legend of a baiting, a pursuit, a hunt, in which a man or god perishes unjustly, mistakenly, perhaps after an unjust trial. It is the one death above all that should not have occurred, and it stirs such profound grief that a lamenting pack forms. Their lament contains the implication that the slain hunter or, even more exalted, savior, has died for the sake of those who mourn him. Up to the formation of the lamenting pack—as against lamenting individuals—the scenario describes the Babylonian legend of Tammuz and Ishtar (Adonis and Aphrodite), and the Egyptian legend of Osiris and Isis. With the coming together of lamenting relatives and disciples into a pack, the complete scenario describes the beginnings of Christianity or of Shiite Islam, founded by Hussein, grandson of the prophet. If there were all told perhaps six hundred Christians at the first Whitsuntide and ten million by the time of Constantine, the core of the religion was (and is) the same: the lament, and not by one or two people but by a group. And this group, this erstwhile hunting or baiting pack, is expiating its guilt by becoming a lamenting pack. Because man continues unable to renounce pack slaying, religions of lament, nicely filling a niche in his psychic makeup, have a bright future.

The founding of Shiite Islam, the official religion of Iran and a strong factor in Iraq and India, follows the above legend structure no less closely than does Christianity. Hussein, would-be caliph, placing too much reliance on fickle supporters of his cause, is surrounded and killed in battle on the tenth day of the month of Muharram. Not only killed; his body contained thirty-three lance thrusts and thirty-four sword cuts. His body is trampled by the hooves of his enemies' horses and beheaded. Islam, Canetti asserts, has all the traits of a religion of war. Even so, the Shiites developed into the world's most extreme religion of lament. A lamenting pack quickly formed, pilgrims whose destination was Hussein's grave, surrounded already by four thousand angels. That stream has continued and multiplied many times over, and especially during the festival that marks the first ten days of the month of Muharram, when the manifestations of expiational guilt are everywhere. By Canetti's reckoning, this "confirm[s] the centrality of lament" (128).

A particularly provocative chapter is "Catholicism and the Crowd." What Canetti calls the "spaciousness" of Catholicism—it has room for everyone—is owing not only to its great age but also to its aversion to potentially violent crowds. More effectively than any secular state it defends itself against the crowd and the threat of the crowd. Its cautiousness toward even the semblance of a crowd is reflected in its penchant for safely distant angelic hosts and, on earth, for ordered and orderly processions and the veneration that such processions imply and assert. The Catholic Church does have its crowd crystals, but these are the religious orders embracing the true Christians, committed, as the laity cannot be, to a life of poverty, chastity, and obedience—a most effective brake on the formation of open crowds.

The last chapter of the third section is devoted to the descent of the Holy Fire on Easter Eve in the Church of the Holy Sepulchre in Jerusalem. Or, more exactly, to the thousands of pilgrims who foregathered there for the event, in the course of which they were transformed from a lament pack to a triumph pack, often enough accompanied by panic and the loss of life.

The fourth section, entitled "The Crowd in History," seems to confirm the author's turn from the didactic inculcation of principles to a more expansive application of those principles, to greater speculation, to increased use of anecdote. The turn has been gradual. There have been speculation and anecdote in the first three sections, and Canetti does not abruptly cease being didactic. But in general the emphasis now lies on application. Typical is the first chapter, "National Crowd Symbols," in which with insight and restrained wit Canetti propounds the appropriate crowd symbol for eight nationalities.

The sea is the crowd symbol for the English. For the French their Revolution is the crowd symbol par excellence. For the Swiss it is their mountains (an elaboration, by way of crowd concept, of an idea frequently used and discussed by Swiss writers). The corrida, with its encircling ring and its execution of the beast, is the crowd symbol for the Spanish. For the Italians, caught in a paralyzing dilemma between the empty Coliseum and the continually filled Church of St. Peter, fascism offered faked antiquity, a false symbol that happily failed. And the crowd symbol for the Jews, despite their great diversity, is that of the moving multitude, as in the Exodus.

In the following chapter, "Inflation and the Crowd," inflation is, again and more elaborately, placed within the rubric of the crowd experience—

and one that, in 1923 and later, the Germans shifted onto the Jews; significantly, not just onto German Jews but onto the moving multitude, onto Jewry worldwide.

Canetti's stand on Marxism is revealed—or at any rate strongly suggested—in a chapter called "Distribution and Increase: Socialism and Production." His stance is distanced, objective, and implicitly critical. However differently the proponents and the adversaries of socialism may think about the distribution of goods, they concur in venerating production—the more the better. "The *hubris* of production goes back to the *increase pack*" (191; italics are Canetti's). The increase in the numbers of the proletariat replicates that of the primitive increase pack. That is, they had more children than others. And they kept migrating from the countryside to the centers of production. No one thought that there should be fewer of them because they led miserable lives, for parallel to their increase would be the increase in production—again a feature of the primitive increase pack. In countries dominated by the proletariat, equitable distribution of production is at least theoretically as important as increase of production. In short, Canetti is keenly aware of the shortcomings of socialism and of its failure to deliver.

"Entrails of Power" is the fifth section of *Crowds and Power*. While Canetti does not abandon his concepts of the crowd, this sectional title accurately suggests that the crowd is no longer in the forefront and that power is. "Seizing and Incorporation"—the title of the first chapter—has to do with the individual psychology of seizing prey, eating it, and incorporating it into oneself. The moment of touching reveals the designs of one body on another, followed by pressure, then grinding. With this sequence superior strength has exercised its power.

Canetti is surely thinking of a primitive type of family when he observes that it is the husband who contributes the food and the wife who prepares it for him. But still, it is the mother who dominates a family. Her power over a young child is absolute. She can keep the child a prisoner and control its movements.

The next section is called "The Survivor," and its first chapter bears the same title. Survival is equated with power. Man's designs on immortality reflect that desire for power. And his horror at the sight of death is always mitigated by satisfaction that it is not he but someone else who has died. Anyone who has fought in a war is familiar with this feeling of superiority. Canetti perhaps exaggerates when he declares that the survivor has a sense of having proved himself the stronger. Actually more prevalent, I believe, is the feeling that he has merely been luckier. In "Survival as a Passion" it is suggested that the pleasure of surviving death leads to an addictive need for greater and greater heaps of dead. "The Ruler as Survivor" presents the Emperor Domitian as a type of the paranoid ruler, playing macabre games with his banquet guests.

In "Forms of Survival" Canetti, in speaking of the Etruscans, touches on a theme that receives vigorous reinforcement in his play *The Numbered*. In the play, we recall, a totalitarian government requires that everyone at birth have a locket placed around his or her neck, the contents of the locket giving the date of birth and the predestined date of death. The Etruscans thought that each city and each race had a predestined number of centuries. The Etruscans had ten centuries. But because the Etruscans believed that the number of years in a century was expansible, if the survivor of each generation lived to be over one hundred years, the nation would survive rather longer than, say, ten times one hundred. While the arithmetic differs, the linking element between the chapter in *Crowds and Power* and the theme of *The Numbered* is the predestination or predetermination of life spans. And in each case an escape is provided.

The same chapter contains a tidy elucidation of Canetti's crowd-oriented point of view as against Freud's characteristically individual point of view (although neither Freud nor Freud's work on mass psychology is named). Canetti puts the question: Is the concept of survival, as he has developed it, the same as what has become known as the instinct of self-preservation? No, he replies. The stress on "self" postulates a solitary and self-sufficient human being, an individual. But "preservation" implies *eating* to stay alive as well as *defending* against attack. Were the creature left to itself, it would supposedly eat a handful of grass and harm no one. A likely tale! For if one hand is reaching for food, the other is fending off attackers. Canetti is ironic, sarcastic—the irony contained, not very subtly, in the summary dismissal, "A peaceful creature indeed!" (250).

A long, primarily anecdotal chapter, "The Survivor in Primitive Belief," demonstrates with what clarity primitive people see the survivor, how effectively they take account of his special position, and how they try to avail themselves of it. Whereas—as subsequent chapters attest more fully—resentment of the dead, whose spirits can, for instance, send an epidemic or blight a crop, is widespread. A visit to a cemetery and the awe we put on display there cover a secret satisfaction, not unlike that (presumably) felt by a military survivor whose comrades have fallen. Headstones bearing witness to a long life arouse in the visitor a desire to emulate the long-lived.

Survivorship is obviously a matter of great importance to Canetti. He has thought about it reflectively and intently; it emerges thematically in his imaginative works, in his autobiography, and it is represented by one of a dozen sections in *Crowds and Power*. In a final chapter in this section, entitled simply "Immortality," he demonstrates that literary immortality, or more generally immortality through works, depends on the works containing "the greatest and purest measure of life" (278). For when the superior writer, having abjured killing, enters the lists a century later he is no longer alive and cannot kill. Then it becomes a question of work versus work. Can there by any doubt that Canetti is speaking of himself here?

At the outset of the next section, "Elements of Power," in a chapter titled "Force and Power," Canetti tries to distinguish between force and power (*Gewalt* and *Macht*). Although he does not invoke linguistic categories, the aspectual ones of momentary versus durative summarize the distinction well—and ultimately suggest that "violence and power" might be the more felicitous translation. The difference can be perceived in two concepts of God. On the one hand are religions such as Islam, whose believers yearn for God's force or violence; on the other are those religions for which God's indwelling power is ample.

The chapter "Question and Answer" is not a questionnaire but a discussion of questioning (and answering) as reflexes of relative degrees of power. All questions are intrusive, and when questions are employed as an instrument of power, the sting is severe and painful. But suppose that the questioner is unsatisfied with the information gleaned and so puts further questions. With each answer the respondent "is forced to reveal more of himself" (285). This assertion is interesting not so much for its insight, which is valid enough, as for its relevance to Canetti's autobiographical reluctance to disclose more of himself, or to reveal himself only under carefully controlled circumstances and in carefully controlled gradations. "Personal freedom consists largely in having a defense against questions" (285).

"Secrecy" is the title of the next chapter. Secrecy, the very core of power, is the ultimate defense against questions. Who invokes secrecy gains respect for preserving it. There is a price to pay, however, for secrecy isolates. Still worse, it inhibits self-transformation; it denies the opportunity for self-transformation because it freezes the fluidity essential to transformation.

In the next section, "The Command," and in its first chapter, "The Command: Flight and Sting," we learn that the original command, from which the whole idea of command derives, was to take flight, the flight-command. Flight being the only avenue of escape from a death sentence, the latter still echoes behind all commands. But commands have become domesticated. Even in the military this is true, although a truly disciplined soldier acts only as commanded and stands always in expectation of a command.

There are two kinds of discipline. Open discipline is that of command, which the soldier constantly expects. Secret discipline is that of promotion. Not promotion in rank, which is only the public manifestation, but a promotion that consists in the secret workings of the accumulated stings of command. Every command that a soldier executes leaves a sting in him. He cannot get rid of the accumulated sting except as he can issue commands to those below him in rank. That is the key. He can change his straitjacketed position, rigidly enforced by cumulative sting, only by being promoted, by being enabled to transfer some of the burden of his sting to those lower in rank. The Mongols enforced an exceedingly strict military discipline. How did they bear it; why did they not break under it? Because they were on horses and transferred the main burden of their accumulated sting onto the creatures inferior in rank to them all, their horses.

A chapter entitled "Negativism in Schizophrenia" shows almost no traces of Freud and a great deal of original dialectic thought. Canetti seizes on the fact that a highly suggestible schizophrenic behaves as if he were part of a crowd. Which is to say, a variety of crowds appear in his imaginings. Why is this so? The schizophrenic is often paralyzed into isolated torment by the extreme burden of his stings. To obtain surcease he succumbs to the illusion of the very opposite of his actual state, namely, the illusion of being in a crowd, often a vast crowd. The sting, formed during the carrying out of a (perhaps imagined, certainly exaggerated) command, is thereby reversed. For a mentally competent person, sting may not be susceptible to such facile reversal. On the contrary, the reversal may take years, a lifetime. A reversal crowd may form to liberate a group of people from their accumulated stings; that is a revolt or a revolution. But observe, just as with the schizophrenic, the crowd purges the sting.

Command derives from the threat of death. In domestic commands that threat may remain implicit for it is combined with reward, for example, the promise of food. In its long history, so Canetti avers, it has become "the most dangerous single element in the social life of mankind" (333). Mankind must have the courage to resist it; its tyranny must be broken, to the point that man's stings are more easily and less traumatically removed.

In the next section Canetti returns, more concentratedly, to "Transformation," one of his most pervasive and important themes. He admits that it is very difficult to grasp. For that reason he approaches it from several angles, the first of which is in conjunction with presentiment among the Bushmen. A Bushman feels in his body that, for example, his grandfather—a long while absent—will soon reappear. How, where does he feel it in his body? In the same place on the younger man's body where his grandfather's body bears the scar of an old wound. The grandfather in fact shows up. Another approach to transformation—in this case transformation for flight—is by way of hysteria, mania, and melancholia. Major hysterical outbreaks are a series of violent transformations for flight. Each such transformation or metamorphosis—Canetti uses Kafka's word *Verwandlung*—represents, or is, an attempt to break away, in a different guise or form. This is the stuff of myths and fairy tales the world over—metamorphosing to flee an enemy.

Similarly myths—and fairy tales as well—dwell on transformation effected by self-increase or self-consumption. In the bandicoot myth from Central Australia, cited at length by Canetti, the great ancestor Karora, having killed and eaten two young bandicoots (ratlike marsupials native to Australia), gives birth through his armpit to three sons, who in turn feed on bandicoots. But since the ancestor figure is a totem, half man, half bandicoot, we are witnessing self-consumption as well as self-increase. In the chapter "Crowds and Transformation in Delirium Tremens" Canetti's crowd consists of the hordes of mice or insects that the alcoholic imagines to be crawling on his body. But they do not cause his transformation; the alcohol does that. Rather the alcoholic fancies himself to be watching them from a distance.

The product of transformation is called the figure (*Figur* in the original German, not *Gestalt*). An end product after the completion of transformation, the figure cannot be further transformed. The Egyptian god Anubis, a man with the head of a jackal, immutable through the millennia in this twofold form, is a figure in the sense proposed by Canetti, as is a mythic ancestor totem, man and animal simultaneously, such as the bandicoot totem among the Australian aborigines. Such figures are end products of the process of transformation.

Should that end product, that end state, be one of exceptional rigidity, then we are dealing with a mask. We seem on firm ground, at least within the limits of Canetti's conceptualizing, for his acoustic mask is a characteristic petrifaction of a person's linguistic resources. Among other things the mask, completely rigid, obscuring the play of facial features, imposes distance between itself and the would-be interlocutor or the spectator. Fixity of form is thus complemented by that of distance. The mask effects separation.

As *Crowds and Power* progresses, the component sections become increasingly loosely organized. Such a section is "Aspects of Power." In its first chapter, "Human Postures and Their Relation to Power," Canetti discusses the relationship to power of the various postures: standing, sitting on a chair, lying, sitting on the ground, and kneeling. For example, the orchestral conductor, on his feet and in action, is a perfect illustration of the expression of power. One recognizes the diminishing potential of the listed postures; by the time we arrive at kneeling, the position of supplication, the power potential is slim indeed—in fact the kneeler is powerless. Of a more cohesive nature is the longer final chapter, "General Paralytics and Their Notions of Greatness." Megalomania in paralytics indicates that their notions of greatness center on growth of two kinds: (1) such a megalomaniac wants his body to grow and he cannot accept that he has reached his limit, and (2) he desires crowds, preferably consisting of millions.

The last section before the epilogue deals with "Rulers and Paranoiacs." They are all survivors, although Canetti mentions that fact almost casually. Following a chapter entitled "African Kings" and another called "A Sultan of Delhi: Muhammad Tughlak," Canetti comes to the case of Daniel Paul Schreber, one-time presiding judge of the Court of Appeals in Dresden— and in his own tortured mind the last survivor in the universe. Having spent seven, almost eight, years (sources vary) in asylums as a paranoiac and been released, Schreber wrote a book, *Denkwürdigkeiten eines Nervenkranken* (1903; *Memoirs of My Nervous Illness,* 1955), which describes his experiences in terms of his delusional system. Freud discusses Schreber's work and affliction at great length,[3] but Canetti glosses the case in a distinctly different manner, with the advantage, so to speak, of having seen the great wars (crowds, war packs) of our century.

In Canetti's version Schreber was convinced that his psychiatrist, in alliance with a pack of conspirators, was plotting to take possession of his soul, to murder his soul. By extension—or in somewhat different terms— the psychiatrist's aim was the destruction of Schreber's reason. (Freud does not essentially differ here.) Or rather, it was *their* aim, that of the psychiatrist *and* his conspiratorial henchmen, for all the phenomena associated with Schreber's illness have something to do with crowds. While mankind was perishing in multiple disasters, Schreber, in accordance with his desire, is left as sole survivor, that is, as the possessor of total power. Paranoia, Canetti observes, is "an *illness of power*" (448).

Schreber felt himself being transformed into a woman. Freud maintains that homosexual predisposition and the father complex are at the heart of Schreber's delusion. Such is not the case, however, according to Canetti. Central to everything, for Schreber, was the perceived crowd attack on his reason—in which, moreover, God was complicit. As a paranoiac Schreber is obsessed with uncovering causal relationships, with finding and unmasking conspirators, up to and including God.

Basing his conclusion on the case of Schreber, Canetti voices his "suspicion" that the same profound urge lies behind paranoia that lies behind all power: "the desire to get other men out of the way so as to be the only one; or, in the milder, and indeed often admitted, form, to get others to help him *beome* the only one" (462). That is, a survivor. Freud, interpreting the Schreber case quite differently, perceives a paranoia behind which lie castration fear, latent homosexuality, and a father complex—matters that Canetti all but ignores. On the basis of their respective interpretations of the Schreber case, Canetti's reaction to Freud's psychology is virtual rejection. But it is a rejection effected more by silent omission than by contention or argument, which in fact are not to be found in Canetti's briefer, hence more selective analysis.

The Schreber case—a paranoiac delusion with one adherent, Schreber himself—is used by Canetti as a bridge to his short, generalizing epilogue, "The End of the Survivor" which is loosely tied to what has preceded. Which of the four different kinds of pack—hunting, war, lamenting, or increase—has come to dominate our age? While the lamenting packs of the great religions of the world find their power diminished and give assent to whatever happens, the increase pack has undergone a colossal and frightening expansion. Capitalism and socialism are rivals in the same faith. But war, no longer effective as a means to rapid increase, is dying out. Its last efflorescence was Nazism. So says Canetti; and if we subtract Vietnam and a few others, he is right.

Even amid secularization, the legacy of the religions of lament, especially Christianity, is great, inexhaustible. For he who dies is made significant by lament. Each person is convinced he ought not to die. But the survivor, however glorified and obeyed, or however paranoid, instills disgust in people. The survivor is not yet extinct, nor will he be until we have the strength to perceive him through his disguises and his glorification.

Terror of a supernatural power has today been transferred to the bomb. Compared with this threat, earlier survivors, that is, conquerors, seem pitifully ineffective: Genghis Khan, Tamerlane, and Hitler seem no more than amateurs. Today's survivor, however, is himself afraid, and his triumph is not apt to be of long duration, maybe a few hours. "Today either everyone will survive or no one" (469). That is, the ruler's inviolate primacy has been broken.

But better than to count on this theorem is to deal with the survivor himself, whose modus operandi is to issue commands—commands that, we recall, imply always the sting of death. That threat is the coin of power. To master power we must confront command. And above all—here Canetti seems to rely more on hope than on prescription—"search for means to deprive it [command] of its sting" (470). In spite of taking final refuge in hope, Canetti is to be admired for bringing his *Crowds and Power* into what used to be called relevance, before that word and concept became trivialized. Our hopefulness, if we have paid some attention to *Crowds and Power*—which is itself not unassailable—will be thoughtful and informed.

## NOTES

1. Elias Canetti, *Crowds and Power,* trans. Carol Stewart (New York: Farrar, Straus, 1984) 468. Subsequent references will be noted parenthetically.

2. See the title of Lothar Hennighaus, *Tod und Verwandlung: Elias Canettis poetische Anthropologie aus der Kritik der Psychoanalyse* (Death and Transformation: Elias Canetti's Poetic Anthropology from the Critical Perspective of Psychoanalysis) (Frankfurt am Main: Peter Lang, 1984).

3. Sigmund Freud, "Psychoanalytic Notes upon an Autobiographical Account of a Case of Paranoia (Dementia Paranoides)," *Collected Papers,* trans. Alix and James Strachey (New York: Basic Books, 1959) 3: 387–470.

# CHAPTER SIX

# Essays and Other Collections: *The Human Province; The Conscience of Words; Earwitness; The Secret Heart of the Clock*

The two principal collections of Canetti's essays are *Die Provinz des Menschen: Aufzeichnungen 1942–1972* and *Das Gewissen der Worte*. The first was published in 1973, the second in 1975. The first was translated in 1978 as *The Human Province*; the second followed a year later as *The Conscience of Words*. The subtitle of *Die Provinz des Menschen* tells us that the gathering of aphorisms contained therein runs from 1942 to 1972. In the case of the second book, the title reflects Canetti's continued concern to use words, to write, conscientiously. Especially to write conscientiously because, as becomes more than clear in his *Voices of Marrakesh*, he does not esteem the written word to be of the same inherent authenticity as the oral word.

Similarly the implications of the title, *The Human Province*, bear examination. Canetti is saying that his aphorisms are within, or perhaps are actually equated with, the province of humanity and that the author is staking claim to that province, that he is part of it—a claim we are not likely to gainsay. The human province is one also notably limited by the omnipotence of death, with which, either in its individual form or in the form of war, he contends probably more concentratedly in these aphorisms and sketches than in any of his other writings.

Yet he has no inflated sense of essayistic importance, referring to the contents of *The Human Province* in his preface as "jottings." Jottings about which he was so "irresponsible" as to never read them again, nor did he change them in any way from their original form. How did these modest jottings originate? Writing them was a "safety valve" for the pressure associated with the long-protracted preliminary work on *Crowds and Power*. We can speculate—though Canetti offers no confirmation in his preface—that the pressures generated by World War II, in 1942 in its fourth year, and by his own exile, then in its seventh year, also contributed to the need of a safety valve. In any case the jottings, arranged according to year, became a part of his regimen. There were actually a lot more of them than the selection that appears in the book.

The "jottings" are aphorisms, observations, reflections about things he has read, and perverse flights of his imagination. A single jotting, even a one-liner, may belong to more than one of the above rubrics. How shall we define, for example, "Things will get better. When? When the dogs rule?"[1] Is this an aphorism, or is it a somewhat shocking flight of imagination? Or is it an aphorism distilled from a bit of daring imagining? Rather than trying to impose classification it may be more rewarding to search for and be sensitive to the element of *Verwandlung,* transformation, change, that lies at the root of not only the short entries but also those of greater length.

The example above reflects also an aphoristic predilection of Canetti that we may not have expected: for animals. Elsewhere he wonders whether animals are guilty of original sin, since they too are obliged to die. This jotting embraces, as do many, death is a very specific way. Whereas in the first-quoted jotting death is only implicit: that of humans being a consensual prerequisite (as in a flight of imagination) before the dogs are asked—by whom?— to take over. Death is a transformation, after all. But Canetti does not indulge it on that account, because it blocks, precludes the kind of transformation or transformational possibilities that he sets store by. In the event, he is concerned, as many jottings make clear, not with death per se but with the overcoming of death. For instance: "To sing? About what? About old, mighty things that are dead. War too will die" (34). Unsurprisingly, World War II inspired Canetti to many reflections on war: War equals death, not glory. If we had to murder each other naked rather than in uniform, would war die?

God fares poorly in the jottings. How could it be otherwise in a being created after man's image? Typical of Canetti's low-keyed blasphemy is: "A God who keeps his Creation a *secret.* 'And lo, it was not good' " (96).

Despite the appellation of *Dichter* (poet, writer) conferred on him by critics, Canetti in a jotting of 1967 disavows its applicability to himself; it no longer attracts him. And why? Probably, he suggests, because the word no longer contains everything that he demands of himself. In short, he has transcended his status as a *Dichter,* transformed himself into something more than a *Dichter,* into a thinker, into the author of *Crowds and Power,* into an anthropologist, a sociologist, a philosopher, a psychologist. *Dichter* is a word that implies great respect. Not every novelist is a *Dichter.* Nor is it a word or a concept that became debased under Nazism (although elsewhere Canetti asserts that it "has seemingly been destroyed").[2] So the concept of transformation as applied to Canetti himself is not far-fetched.

It should not be imagined that every Canetti jotting in *The Human Province* is a model of pithy insight and pronouncement. Some have been overtaken by time and events; some suffer from the absence of contextual knowledge on the part of the reader; some simply fall flat. Yet on the whole they comprise an attractive access not only to the way Canetti looks at the human province but also to Canetti himself. One can profitably browse through them before undertaking, say, *Crowds and Power.*

## The Conscience of Words

*The Conscience of Words* is quite different, although it is no less subject to the same critical cavil: namely, that subjectivity and relativism prevail. But if one may not be subjective and relativistic in essays, where could it be more appropriate for a writer of prose? *The Conscience of Words* is a collection of fifteen (originally fourteen) essays from the years 1936 to 1974, presented in the order in which they were written. There is a gap of twenty-six years between the first and the second, but Canetti assures us that the gap is merely chronological, that many of the essays hark back to his earlier experiences and preoccupations. The whole sequence strikes him as a summary of the "spiritual" stages of his adult life—of his various transformations, one might say.

The first essay is a speech given in Vienna in November 1936 in honor of the Austrian novelist Hermann Broch's [*The Sleepwalkers, The Death of Virgil*] fiftieth birthday. Canetti extrapolates from Broch's half-century to a theoretical full century and speculates, under the implicit aura of one's contention with death, that if a man is "very lucky" he will grow to that age. Then, seguing from Broch's years to his profession, he opposes the notion that a great writer is above his time. No, a true writer (like Broch) is in thrall to his time.

How do we identify a true writer? First, he is original. Second, with an urge toward universality he aims to sum up his age, as Broch does in the trilogy, *The Sleepwalkers,* dwelling on the decay of values over the period 1888–1918. And third, a writer has to stand against his time, for time "mollycoddles" death. Now Canetti abruptly changes the topic to *air*—he italicizes the word—to breath. And Broch's vice, his passion, is breathing; he is gifted with something approaching a memory for breath, by which Canetti means the subtle psychology of self-observation and inner experi-

79

ence. This is what gives Broch his artistic power, his diversity. But breathing has no defenses, and Broch is already breathing and choking on the poison—gas warfare here stands for war in general—that will do us all in.

The title of the essay "Power and Survival" (1962) naturally reminds us of Canetti's major work, *Crowds and Power,* much of which is oriented to survival—as, for that matter, is much of Canetti's work, generally speaking. For, to quote a line from the essay, "Survival is at the core of everything that we . . . call power."[3] Stated in another way, the survival situation is "the central situation of power" (16). In a way familiar to us from *Crowds and Power,* Canetti quotes specialized anthropological scientific literature to support his contention. The thought of power naturally takes him to the thought of war, and to the real purpose of war: mass killing—the more corpses the better. He speculates that those who return alive from war contribute to the general sense of invulnerability that enables us to forget or transform the unspeakable horrors of war.

Toward the end of the essay Canetti turns to the case of Daniel Paul Schreber, the former presiding appeals court judge in Dresden. Schreber's mental illness is given far more extensive treatment in *Crowds and Power.* In the present essay Canetti emphasizes the ideas that were fundamental to Schreber's madness. First, the patient believes he is the only human being in the world to survive the catastrophic end of mankind. And second, he is the leader (by virtue of his uniqueness) of myriad souls who cluster about him and who are reduced—literally reduced to minuscule dimensions—by him. It is illuminating that even in a brief three-page summary of the Schreber case, Canetti finds room to denounce Freud's interpretation of the case (dementia paranoides), including the style of writing—"groping"—in which Freud couched his remarks.

Canetti discusses his intellectual relationship to Karl Kraus in "Karl Kraus: The School of Resistance" (1965). He tells how he first came into contact with Kraus in 1924, how Kraus, with his blending of morality and literature, captivated Canetti for a decade, and how Canetti freed himself. All of this was a long time ago—which, as Canetti observes, affords him some perspective. Kraus's principal weapons were literalness and horror. The former was deployed in his technique of readily and accurately employing an adversary's quotations against that adversary. And of horror he was the master, imbuing his listeners with it as he read from, say, his *The Last Days of Mankind.*

What did Canetti learn from Kraus? First, a feeling of absolute responsibility. Second, to keep his ears open, to really listen to the voices about him, and not just the intellectual voices. And what, finally, brought Canetti to rebel against Kraus? It was the wall, the impregnable wall with which Kraus buttressed himself and his arguments; the wall that became an end in itself. Upon his wall of impregnability Kraus arrogated all judging to himself. No one else might judge.

"Dialogue with the Cruel Partner" (1965) isn't really a dialogue but a discussion of a writer's relationship to his diary. Canetti begins by sorting out "notes" and "memo books" from the concept "diary." Notes are spontaneous and contradictory. Memo books—filled or partially filled calendars—are the origin of diaries, and many writers combine the two. Different, however, from a memo book, in a diary the writer talks to himself. And the "fictional *I*"—Canetti's term for the person whom the diarist addresses—really listens, really challenges. He is always present, he cannot leave. He is both patient and malicious. The authorial *I*, the diary, has its own obsessions and problems; Canetti mentions especially that of obstinacy vis-à-vis the fictional *I*. As with Kafka it is always and again the same thing that keeps bothering him. Finally, the enigma of transformation is writ large in a diary, at least in one that is written over some extensive period, such as a lifetime.

Also from 1965 is the short essay "Realism and New Reality." Canetti contends—his essayistic method is not to suggest but to self-confidently contend—that total literary reality usually proved an unrealistic goal (Zola was naïve). Past reality makes us feel helpless. The change to contemporary—but Canetti avoids any adjective here—reality embodies three essential aspects: increasing reality, a more precise reality, and the reality of the future. The first seems to equate with what we nowadays call the knowledge explosion. The second stresses the impact of scientific precision and scientific method. The third embraces utopias as well as the dark side of the future. One or more of these aspects of reality must emerge in the contemporary novel.

By far the most extensive and quite likely the most-often cited Canetti essay is "Kafka's Other Trial: The Letters to Felice" (1969). It consists of genial and expansive commentary on Kafka's letters to his fiancée and on topics suggested or inspired by the letters. The point of view is conspicuously sympathetic to Kafka, whose story "The Metamorphosis" ("Die Verwandlung") served as a structural and thematic model for Canetti. For the most part Canetti is less sympathetic to Felice, although he manages an indulgent, perhaps slightly amused toleration of her. It's a difficult if permissive (critics fault him for that reason) role that Canetti assumes; difficult because the death of a love affair on the shoals of misunderstanding and incompatibility is in essence not very amusing.

He notes early on the contrast in parental attitudes in the Kafka household and in that of Kafka's friend Max Brod (where Kafka was introduced to the Brod kinswoman, Felice Bauer from Berlin). Max Brod's parents were proud of their son's writing accomplishments, and they took his literary friends—Kafka was that and more—very seriously. Kafka felt comfortable in the Brod home and had to be all but kicked out, in a friendly way, when bedtime came.

Canetti is impressed by Felice's quick change from the borrowed slippers of Mrs. Brod to her own boots. A swift and admirable transformation. With Kafka, on the other hand, any transformation is a slow process. He is slow and indecisive. Even his courtship of Felice begins, as Kafka himself admits, with indecisiveness, which leads Canetti to pose the contrast: Franz indecisive and weak, Felice efficient and healthy.

One may here interpose that Kafka as a writer was quite decisive. Two nights after his first letter to Felice he writes "Das Urteil" ("The Judgment") in one swoop and dedicates it to her—a feat of composition he does not repeat, to be sure, but still it seems a rather decisive action. From that a week later he turns to "The Stoker," the first chapter of *America*, but published separately as a novella; in two more months five more chapters of *America*; during a two-week break within those two months "The Metamorphosis." Canetti has an answer. All literary productivity, he asserts, is conditional, and Kafka during this period was conditioned by his feeling that Felice expected something of him. But in reality, Canetti continues, she was an uncomplicated person—proved by Kafka's citations from her letters.

Those who admire the grace and irony and integrity and the highly disciplined writing of Kafka's Austrian contemporary, Arthur Schnitzler, will not be pleased by Canetti's pinpointing of Kafka's antipathy toward Schnitzler. Was it perhaps jealousy occasioned by Felice's desire to go to the theater to see Schnitzler's drama, *Professor Bernhardi*? Kafka does not want to be dragged to the theater to see "poor literature, which is what Schnitzler largely represents to me." He goes on: "For I do not like Schnitzler at all. . . . His big plays and his big prose are filled . . . with a simply staggering mass of the most repugnant hackwork. One cannot put him down deeply enough" (71). To be sure, Kafka does allow to Felice that some of Schnitzler's works are "partly excellent." Canetti is moved to conclude that this display of aggressive jealousy of another writer by Kafka was part and parcel of his attachment to Felice.

There are very few writers, says Canetti, who are totally themselves. One such was Kafka. The critic should therefore adhere closely to Kafka's own statements. Sound enough critical advice, but lacking the essential proviso that an author is not necessarily the best critic of his own work.

According to Canetti, Kafka's preoccupation with his own body was determined by his skinniness. Thence—here I'm extending Canetti's reasoning—Kafka's frequent preoccupation with smallness. Naturally Kafka felt demolished at the "trial" to which he was subjected by Felice's family at Askanischer Hof, the hotel he stayed at in Berlin. The aspersions or charges bore on his dubious attitude about the engagement with Felice. He reacted with obduracy to being made to feel tiny, while his accusers, Felice's family, loomed as giants. The central point of Canetti's essay is: After the termination of the first engagement between Franz and Felice, the ensuing two years of correspondence between them came to seem like a trial, which was transformed into the other, literary *Trial*. Canetti declares that the emotional content of the original betrothal, which took place in the Bauer home, and the "trial" six weeks later at Askanischer Hof, which ended the first engagement, "passed directly into *The Trial*" (100). Further, the "almost inextricable situation at the betrothal has thus been exposed in the first chapter of *The Trial*" (102). A rather sweeping statement, though not without insight, a Kafka scholar might reply.

To return to the subject of smallness, of diminishment, Canetti speaks of animals. Paraphrasing Canetti, who seems in *The Human Province* to be partial to dogs: You have to have small animals at eye-level to see them accurately. Bending down condescends; raising them to eye-level magnifies. That recalls Kafka's—and his protagonist's—magnification of the bug in "The Metamorphosis" or the narrative magnification of the molelike animal in "The Burrow." This is all in the course of Canetti's long digression from the Franz/Felice nexus, which has the effect of suggesting structurally the temporary freezing or nonexistence of their relationship between the termination of the first engagement and the prelude to the second. The overall gist of the excursus is the thematic nature of power, powerlessness, humiliation, and transformation in Kafka—not a startling formulation, but a neat one.

The resumption of the affair between Kafka and Felice—which became, for a few days in Marienbad, a genuine love affair—is foredoomed, as Canetti's commentary makes clear. By 1917 the flow of letters that had begun in 1912 has just about stopped. Felice's September visit to Kafka and his sister Ottla on the latter's farm at Zürau was a disaster. Ten days later

Kafka, not even opening her letters to him, wrote his next-to-final letter to her, disagreeable and defensive. The last is on October 16, distanced and cold, an unmistakable if implicit warning to her not to return. Canetti draws no grand final inferences or conclusions. His quotations and text give the impression that Felice was the more deeply hurt of the pair, but his sympathy for her is spare and distant—like Kafka's.

"Word Attacks: Address at the Bavarian Academy of the Fine Arts" dates from 1969. Basing himself on his linguistic situation as a German-language author living in England, Canetti notes the tendency of German to seem odder and odder; more and more of its characteristics became increasingly conspicuous to him. But then the second language, English, becomes increasingly banal, while the first defends itself. He finds himself filling page after page with German words—not sentences, just words, having nothing to do with what he was working on. He fancies that the words are getting back at him, thus the "word attacks" in his title. While he views his role in the word attacks in a pathological light, that role is in fact simply unavoidable under the all-out pressure mustered by English on its home territory. But the man of today is compelled to seek a private sphere, and *his* private sphere is the German language.

"Hitler, According to Speer: Grandeur and Permanence" (1971) is a gloss of the Hitler who appears in the *Memoirs* of Albert Speer.[4] Speer was Hitler's architect, confidant, and finally denouncer. Speer, and Canetti in turn, find that Hitler's grandiose architectural plans slated for implementation in the year 1950 are unforgettable, owing to their flagrant irrevelancy to modern architecture. Hitler's buildings had to be bigger than those of any predecessor, not only as befits a conqueror but also as befits a mind dominated and dedicated to the concept of the crowd. It is the preoccupation with the crowd that brings Hitler into Canetti's special purview. The buildings, like the pyramids of Egypt, are to be permanent, "the symbol of the crowd that cannot crumble" (148).

These buildings are to outstrip, outdo all others, a mad notion that pervaded Hitler's paranoiac mind, fueling his insatiable need for victories even as his own cities were sinking into ruins. (Hitler planned to firebomb London; ironically the strategy of firebombing was successfully adopted by his enemies.) But that was not before Hitler had amply indulged his own typically paranoiac linking of permanence and destruction (a linkage well documented in the case of Daniel Paul Schreber). Hitler had ever been attuned to crowds; yet with the bombing of his own cities he did not allow himself—as did Churchill—to be seen among the crowds of those who had been bombed out. For Hitler, another crowd grew acute: the Jews. Already enslaved, they were now to be exterminated.

To this end this "empiricist of the crowd" allowed delusion and reality to overlap. Thus the prolongation of the war and the absurd defense of Berlin appeared justifiable to Hitler's deluded mind because Franklin Roosevelt's death shortly earlier had presaged a turning point in the war. In Hitler's mind, his model, Frederick the Great, had been similarly saved by the death of the Empress Elizabeth of Russia. Canetti is at his argumentive best in relating the calculated infamies (and the presumably uncalculated stupidities) of Hitler to his crowd theory. He makes a most convincing case, and the reader can enjoy watching him sink his polemic teeth into the late dictator.

"Confucius in His Conversations" (1971) is a series of Canetti's aperçus of Confucius and his wisdom. He is impressed by Confucius's lack of success, by his ignoring power in favor of interest in the possibilities of power. He is equally impressed by Confucius's love of study, by his admiration for the man who does not act with calculation. The *Conversations* of Confucius presents a man who is above all a model to be emulated. But counter-models as well are presented. Canetti, obsessed as he is by death and its defeat, knows of no sage who took death as seriously as Confucius. The man who mourns the prescribed three years for his father, Canetti believes, will be purged of his lust for survival. No civilization but that of Confucius makes such an earnest attempt to wipe out that lust.

Canetti concludes "Tolstoy: The Final Ancestor" (1971) with a comparison between on the one hand Tolstoy and his wife and on the other hand Canetti's fictional couple in *Auto-da-Fé*, Peter Kien and Therese Krumbholz. Canetti relates some of his resonances to Tolstoy's life (not to his works, for they sometimes contain boring things). Tolstoy's incredible self-identification with Christ makes the latter a crutch in Tolstoy's pursuit of his own transformation into a peasant. Tolstoy sees through and rejects power in every form. It is especially painful for Canetti to see a man of such incorruptible character then make a sort of pact with death. Having survived the deaths of most of the young members of his family, Tolstoy would be horrified to learn that—according to Canetti's theory—his sense of life is thereby strengthened. And Tolstoy's is a *complete* life (Canetti's italics) until the final moment—including the flight from his wife shortly before his death.

Toward the end Tolstoy and his wife are as far apart as Kien and Krumbholz. And having lived long together they knew more about each other.

They had children; Tolstoy had disciples; the stage is not so barren as Kien's apartment. While Tolstoy would probably have seen his wife as Therese, he would never have identified himself with Kien.

"Dr. Hachiya's Diary of Hiroshima" (1971) is an admiring look at the physician and his diary that covers the fifty-six days after the dropping of the atomic bomb on that city. Most of all it is Hachiya's unfailing respect for the dead—cremated nightly outside his hospital—that attracts Canetti's admiration. Hachiya believes that it was not the emperor but the officers' corps that bore responsibility for the war with the United States, a judgment that Canetti implicitly accepts. But while Canetti is tough-minded and knowledgeable about the European phase of World War II, he inclines here to a kind of sentimental defensiveness in the case of Japan and Dr. Hachiya, who was indignant at the lack of respect shown the dead in Hiroshima. Canetti justified the firebombing of German cities because Hitler had the idea (but not the means) to firebomb London. Yet in his excoriation of those who destroyed Hiroshima, it seems not to occur to Canetti to consider the Japanese atrocities in the Philippines and elsewhere.

Canetti begins "Georg Büchner: Speech at the Awarding of the Georg Büchner Prize" (1972) with the candid admission that he is no connoisseur of the writings of that revolutionary German author who after flight from Germany and refuge in Strasbourg died at the age of twenty-three in Zurich. Canetti recounts that he was emerging from a year devoted to *Auto-da-Fé*, perhaps feeling guilty for having allowed his fictional Peter Kien to burn books, when he read Büchner's play *Woyzeck* one night in August 1931. Veza, his wife-to-be, had recommended it to him, and now she recommended Büchner's novella *Lenz* as well. Canetti modestly remarks that, proud as he was of *Auto-da-Fé*, it seemed smaller after he had read *Lenz*.

Strasbourg, an "open world" in which for two years Büchner breathed freedom, was very much the "breeding ground of a new German literature" (194): Herder and Goethe in their youth, and now Büchner, who learns easily to move about in French. Even so, the terror of the German prison he had fled never leaves him, as is to be seen in his tragedy *Danton's Death*. But it is his *Woyzeck* that scores what Canetti terms "the most perfect upset in literature"—a feat now taken for granted—"the discovery of the lowly" (201).

The essay that Canetti calls "The First Book: *Auto-da-Fé*" (1973) contains the chief autobiographical details attendant on the writing of the novel. In early drafts Peter Kien was designated as B., standing for "Book Man," for at that time he had no other quality than that of books. The next designation, Brand (conflagration), contained not his primary quality but his end. Brand became Kant, and Kant became Kien (resinous kindling).

The model for Kien's housekeeper and then wife was Canetti's landlady on Hagenberg Street in Hacking, outside of Vienna, during the six-year period dating from April 1927. Though the landlady's skirt was not blue, it did reach the floor; and like her literary descendant Therese Krumbholz she held her head at an angle. The first speech Canetti heard from her is, on Canetti's word, reproduced verbatim in *Auto-da-Fé*. Not just the figure and character of Krumbholz derive from Canetti's residency on Hagenberg Street. From his room he had a view of Steinhof, an institution housing six thousand insane patients.

At the time of the burning of the Palace of Justice, 15 July 1927, Canetti's idolization of Karl Kraus was at its zenith. But in fall 1930, when he had just completed the eighth chapter of *Auto-da-Fé*, Kafka's "The Metamorphosis" fell into his hands. "This purest of all models" (211), though impossible of attainment, did lend strength to Canetti.

When he finished a version of the novel in October 1931, so Canetti confesses, he sent it, three heavy volumes in a huge package, to Thomas Mann (together with a haughty and dignified letter) for a collegial reading. A few days later the volumes were returned, unread, Mann declaring to the wounded author that he lacked the strength. But there is a happy sequel to the tale. Some four years later, when *Auto-da-Fé* was published, Mann read it and praised it both intelligently and flatteringly.

"The New Karl Kraus: Speech Given at the Berlin Academy of the Arts" (1974) is a tribute to the Kraus whom Canetti had ceased to idolize—his idolization had lasted five years, followed by four years of an increasingly critical attitude. Kraus, editor and writer of his own journal, *Die Fackel* (The Torch), was a murderous—the word is Canetti's—satirist, the greatest German satirist (Canetti does not here distinguish German from Austrian). But Kraus's very evenness, very consistency of assault, in *Die Fackel* makes it unbearable. Still, says Canetti, Kraus was the only literary person to oppose World War I from the start. (In fact, Arthur Schnitzler also opposed it from the beginning.) The war is the stuff of Kraus's vast and powerful satirical tragedy, *The Last Days of Mankind*, the peak of his creative career.

The "new" Karl Kraus referred to in Canetti's title dates from the publication of his letters to Sidonie von Nádhérny in 1974. Kraus was introduced to her on 8 September 1913, and his letters to her cover the last twenty-three years of his life. Canetti's aim, however, is to familiarize us

87

with the first two of those years, when the letters reveal that Kraus identified completely with Sidi, that he drew from her a sense of unity without which the completion of what is conceivably the world's most extensive and potent denunciation of war could not have been. In Canetti's admiration of *The Last Days of Mankind* we feel his own implacable hatred of war as much as an echo of his former idolization of Kraus.

In a preface to *The Conscience of Words* Canetti explains that the last essay, "The Writer's Profession," was added to the original collection to serve as a conclusion—previously lacking—that "wraps it up from the inside" (ix). The speech of the same name was given in Munich in January 1976; afterward he came to realize that it comprised a fitting ending to *The Conscience of Words*. Not for the first time he expresses his concern—here more like misgivings—about recent implications of the German word *Dichter,* a writer or poet. He wonders if it can be rescued from destruction and again imbued with honor as well as obligation.

In "The Writer's Profession" he contests the notion commonly propounded that literature is dead, heaping scorn on those who accordingly abjured the word *Dichter* and proclaimed themselves simply "people who write." Such a writer as well as one who still "self-complaisantly" calls himself a *Dichter* share Canetti's mistrust equally. In the first place, literature is by no means dead, and in the second place, no one today can be a *Dichter* unless he entertains serious doubts about his right to be one.

Canetti offers a quote from an anonymous author, dated 23 August 1939, one week before World War II was unleashed: "But everything is over. If I were really a writer, I would have to be able to prevent the war" (237). How preposterous—our initial reaction—that any writer should imagine he has such power. But another interpretation is possible: the anonymous author, however irrationally, is admitting responsibility; he is accusing himself rather than the real bearers of the responsibility. It is this irrational claim to responsibility that captivates Canetti and sets him to thinking. What *can* a *Dichter* do? Or first, what must he forbid himself? He must not approach reality with scorn; he must not deny any connection to reality, must not cultivate an inner remoteness from what takes place.

And what positive steps must be taken? Here we approach the heart of Canetti's contention, and we are not overly surprised that he casts it in his own terms, that he turns to one of his principal themes. The *Dichter* must be the keeper of metamorphosis, or in its Latinate form, transformation. The practice of the true *Dichter* includes experience of the most disparate people, whom he understands "in an ancient, pre-scholarly way" (243). That precludes Freudian psychology, we may confidently assume, for what Canetti is driving at is, precisely, metamorphosis, transformation. Encountering people and—in a very Canettian turn of phrase—"absorb[ing] them alive" (243): that is metamorphosis. The true *Dichter* appropriates earlier metamorphoses through wide reading; contemporary ones he absorbs or appropriates by means of his openness to people around him.

Metamorphoses contain myths. The essence of myths is the metamorphoses that occur in them. But unfortunately myths have been so debased in our age that they are felt to be lies and are discarded. Such a debasement of myth—the worst instances are those perpetrated by science—is accomplished by psychoanalysis, which, so Canetti asserts, draws much of its strength from the myth of Oedipus. People need reeducation, not in such spurious appropriations as that of psychoanalysis but in the archetypal images to be found in myths. Thus Canetti's fundamental agreement with Jung. Enhanced appreciation of myth by the readers of a *Dichter* enables the latter to more easily fulfill his responsibility to effect metamorphosis. And, to reiterate, to be a *Dichter* a person must feel responsibility. A responsibility for life—now destroying itself—is nourished by compassion. The lives that enter him by metamorphosis or transformation give him also—this is vintage Canetti—the strength to oppose death. For the task of the *Dichter* is anything but that of handing mankind over to death. If he seeks nothingness, it is only to find and blaze a trail out of it.

## Earwitness

*Earwitness: Fifty Characters* is not a book of essays but a gathering of satirical character sketches. It is a slim book. Each satire portrays a particularly flawed example of contemporary humankind in two or three or four trenchant paragraphs. The topics run from "The Loser," the man who is always losing everything, to "The Fun-Runner," the vapid jet-setter compulsively hopping planes from one airport to another.

The title satire, "The Earwitness"—observe again Canetti's penchant for titular sense organs—occurring just short of midway in the book, provides an especially ominous illustration. In making no effort to look, the Earwitness hears all the better, huddling in a corner, ever unobtrusive. When it comes time for him to blurt out what he has overheard, his physical stature actually appears to increase. He spills all: indecencies of every kind, lies, obscure invectives, even things he doesn't understand. His is a unique gift. Like Pontius Pilate ("What I have written I have written"), "Whatever he [the Earwitness] has heard, he has heard,"[5]and not even God can change it.

But the Earwitness has a human side too. Like ordinary folk he takes vacations, in his case by clapping "blinders" (earplugs?) on his ears; he no longer slinks, he looks people right in the eye, a friendly sort, amenable to having a sociable drink. When he is in this hail-fellow-well-met guise, his conversation partners have no idea that they are conversing with the executioner himself, with him who otherwise holds life-and-death power over one! How incredibly innocent people are, goes Canetti's closing observation, when no one is eavesdropping. Whereupon the reader adds: and how guilty otherwise!

In Canetti as elsewhere it's a thin line between satire that works and satire that doesn't work. It must be admitted that not all of it works in *Earwitness*. The humor tends toward what Americans imagine to be a British cast: understated or even unstated. There are few *pointes* or punch lines. Further, the titles are often so recondite as to be baffling. "The Long-Changer" is an overchanger, as of money, the opposite of a shortchanger. "The Beauty-Newt," called bewt for short, is a man excessively devoted to aestheticism. Translated puns have a habit of falling flat, although that is not Canetti's doing. Canetti's thematic preoccupations are less apt to bear familiar names when in satiric dress. But both transformation and death are quietly represented in "The Earwitness." The Earwitness transforms himself while on vacation. But he remains "the executioner."

## The Secret Heart of the Clock

*The Secret Heart of the Clock: Notes, Aphorisms, Fragments, 1973–1985* is a translation of a similarly curiously titled German collection of 1987, *Das Geheimherz der Uhr*. If this title does not refer—as many of Canetti's titles do—to a sense organ, at least it refers to a highly important, more central bodily organ. Actually the title derives from an aphorism within the book: "Unknown to all, the secret heart of the clock."[6] We may take that to refer, first, to the theme of time and aging—the author's aging—fairly prominent but in no way dominant in the "notes, aphorisms, fragments." Second, it bespeaks a self-analysis of somewhat more intensity than we are used to encountering in Canetti.

The book is arranged according to year, and the entries range in length from one or two lines to, rarely, two or three pages. More frequently than in the earlier *Earwitness,* the entries overtly reflect the familiar concerns and gambits of Canetti, including occasional quotations from other writers.

Public life, says Canetti, "robs a person of his integrity. Is there still a possibility of public truth?" (5). Probably not, we may reply, if one thinks of recent politicians—and it's likely that Canetti was. But the same pronouncement and question, differently oriented, can also be profitably considered in the light of Canetti's own disposition to avoid public life.

"He who is obsessed by death is made guilty by it" (6). Canetti, despite the blurb on the jacket, is not given to "guiltily gloomy meditation on death." Rather he is given to a nonguilty struggle against death.

Back to Karl Kraus, by whom Canetti feels "withered" (16). Kraus's lengthy sentences, his "armored sentences" of condemnation, nevertheless lack an over-all goal. They contain no knowledge. Kraus has no interest in knowledge because he can't condemn knowledge. What Kraus does is to *see through.* As we know, Kraus opposed World War I from its inception, for which Canetti earlier lauded him highly. But now he informs us that such an activity cannot avoid pathos—perhaps "legitimate pathos" (17), but still pathos.

Canetti admits to having less credibility than Kafka. Why? The answer is pure Canetti. Because he's been living for so long. But he feels that younger writers look to him to help "against the scourge of death in literature." Well they might; his "contempt for death grows with each year" (21).

Another note lends support to the inference that Canetti's active contempt for death derives from the boy Canetti's having been robbed of his father by death. He finds meaningless any picture of his father, unbelievable any written word of his father. Yet "in me he was always more for being dead" (22).

Canetti marvels at how Goethe *distributes* himself, at how Goethe repeatedly escaped the periodization of his life, launching his transformations in such a way as to make full use of them.

Repeatedly Canetti condemns human cruelty to animals. And frequently he refers to conversations with "the child," that is, his young daughter. Although the reference is simply to "her," it is undoubtedly Johanna. He asks her if she would like to understand animal language. No, she wouldn't. Why not? Her answer: "So they won't be afraid" (43).

Not to be outdone by those Americans who distrust former President Nixon, Canetti observes that whereas the satellite picture of the active volcano on Jupiter's moon makes it seem real, hauling Nixon's picture to the earth's moon made the moon landing "untrustworthy" (60).

91

Leafing through the issues of Karl Kraus's journal *Die Fackel* covering the period that Canetti calls his "slave years"—his years of idolizing Kraus—he is seized by horror. It is as though he has been released from bondage (64).

Returning to his favorite writer after Kafka, the revolutionary Georg Büchner, Canetti declares that Büchner "has the greatest concentration" (101), meaning, evidently, that Büchner gets the most information and allusion into a single, not necessarily long sentence. For each Büchner sentence is new to Canetti even though he knows the sentence.

Canetti quotes the Mexican novelist and short-story writer, Juan Rulfo, most famous for his masterpiece novel *Pedro Páramo*, on death: "Death in Mexico is not a sacred and alien thing. Death is the most ordinary thing there is" (114). We infer that next to having no death at all, next to prevailing over death, is death relegated to the rank of "the most ordinary thing."

In reflecting on his *Crowds and Power* Canetti judges that its form will prove to be its strength. Had he continued it, he would have destroyed it with his hopes. As it is, he obliges "the readers to search for *their* hopes" (115).

To summarize, in *The Secret Heart of the Clock* Canetti in his eighties is a bit more revelatory of himself than usual. His themes are the familiar ones of transformation and overcoming death, the latter now predominating. He is deeply concerned about nuclear annihilation, or human destruction of the earth by one means or another, including the destruction of animals by humans. His literary interests are compellingly broad. Karl Kraus, with whose thoughts he came to terms decades ago, remains nonetheless prominent in his mind. Canetti's acerbic perceptivity has not diminished with the increase in his years. On the other hand his notations describing "the child," his daughter, are charmingly perceptive.

## NOTES

1. Elias Canetti, *The Human Province*, trans. Joachim Neugroschel (New York: Farrar, Straus, 1986) 60. Subsequent references will be noted parenthetically.
2. Elias Canetti, *The Conscience of Words*, trans. Joachim Neugroschel (New York: Farrar, Straus, 1984) ix.
3. *The Conscience of Words*, 14. Subsequent references will be noted parenthetically.
4. Albert Speer, *Inside the Third Reich: Memoirs*, trans. Richard and Clara Winston (New York: Macmillan, 1969).

5. Elias Canetti, *Earwitness: Fifty Characters*, trans. Joachim Neugroschel (New York: Farrar, Straus, 1986) 44.

6. Elias Canetti, *The Secret Heart of the Clock*, trans. Joel Agee (New York: Farrar, Straus, 1989) 120. Subsequent references will be noted parenthetically.

# CHAPTER SEVEN

# The Voices of Marrakesh

The German subtitle of *The Voices* is *Aufzeichnungen nach einer Reise*: "Essays after a Trip." The subtitle of the English translation, however, is *A Record of a Visit*, which creates the unfortunate impression—and one that has achieved critical respectability—that we are dealing here with a more-or-less conventional travel diary. Because a traditional travel diary, a "record," is hardly what one would expect of Canetti, forming a rather radical contrast to the rest of his work, it may be profitable to focus our attention on what the German subtitle, "Essays after a Trip," really says and implies.

Not essays *about* a trip, nor essays *on* a trip, but essays *after* a trip. Why is the reference to time, and what is its implication? Before an answer is offered, it is probably relevant to know that when he wrote *The Voices of Marrakesh*, Canetti had come to an impasse with *Crowds and Power*, which he had been working on for the better part of two decades. Without inventing psycho-biographic details, we may still relevantly speculate about how he may have felt as he packed for his North African sojourn, and unpacked on his return.

The fourteen sketches that comprise *Voices* are not a "record" but a well-developed sequential literary structure. They were written not during Canetti's visit to Morocco but shortly after his return to Europe. The date is 1954. He did not publish them then. It was 1967 before he let himself be persuaded to publish them. "After" seemed the appropriate preposition. Its implication is distance, temporal distance, but artistic and literary distance too, with all that that suggests in the way of literary strategy and fashioning. In a word, these were no hastily jotted, unrevised notes composed, say, in the tumult of a marketplace.

Yet Canetti asserts in a letter of 4 January 1969 that the essays developed (note that his point of view is that of the essays) "easily and quickly."[1] Therefore he doesn't attach much importance to them; he esteems only what takes him a lot of time and costs him a lot of preparation. Authors, however, are not necessarily the keenest critical guides to their own work. We can hold the matter in abeyance as we examine *The Voices of Marrakesh* and come to see, I think, that although brief, it is no light work and that it is closely bound up with themes that we recognize as characteristic of Canetti.

The "voices" in *The Voices of Marrakesh* suggests immediately to the attentive reader that he or she is dealing with an integral part of the Canetti biographical and critical canon. For like *The Tongue Set Free*, *The Torch in My Ear*, and *Earwitness*, we have to do with a titular reference to an auditory image, to oral language, and we are as well reminded of the acoustic mask prominent in the early dramas and in *Auto-da-Fé*. It would be misleading to suggest that *Voices* is permeated by auditory images, yet they are numerous and generally significant, and the careful reader will be sensitive to their occurrence and their importance.

Marrakesh, which nowadays usually appears in atlases as Marrakech, is a sizable city in Morocco some two hundred miles south of Casablanca, thus inland and close to the Atlas Mountains, to which Canetti makes brief reference. It is noteworthy that Canetti has so subtly and so ambiguously worked the role of the city into his narratives that the most remarkable critical disagreement exists concerning the importance of that role. Whereas in the view of one critic Canetti is not writing "about" Marrakesh, in the opinion of another, Marrakesh is the actual protagonist of the fourteen short tales.[2] Besides the role of the city, another, equally important point to keep in mind is that each story can stand alone as a fully developed unit, while at the same time it comprises part of a larger entity, namely, the fourteen taken as a whole. To best appreciate this structural and narrative nicety one should if possible read *Voices* from start to finish in one sitting.

*Voices* is narrated by an authorial *I* who shares key characteristics with Canetti. But the narrator's detachment is probably greater than what one expects of Canetti, giving the impression that he is rather more English than Central European—but speaking French, the lingua franca of educated Arabs, and taking quiet pride in his Jewishness and his ultimate consanguinity with Moroccan Jews, to whom he feels drawn. As one tale segues to another the narrator learns how to better understand a thoroughly non-European culture, how to make his way in it. Because time—temporal distance—forms such an important part of the background of *Voices*, we are not surprised that the authorial *I* narrates from a distinctly temporal perspective, that, for example, he often inserts a temporal hiatus before the resolution of the story. The authorial *I* complements his aurally and visually observational viewpoint with a psychological viewpoint. That is, he asks questions about the welter of strange customs that he observes— sometimes an all but overwhelming welter—while at other moments he proves instinctively, subjectively, in tune with the strange sensations, with objectively unfamiliar modes of human reaction.

This mixture of astonishment with emotional perception is everywhere present. For instance, in the introductory story, "Encounters with Camels," the narrator is at first keen to visit the camel market in Marrakesh and prevails upon a friend to drive him there, where they encounter a single rabid camel, shrieking, destined, according to the broken French of their informant, for the slaughterhouse. The atmosphere is charged with fear, mostly emanating from the doomed beast. A sad scene—the first of three, in the course of which the narrator progressively synthesizes his perceptiveness with his astonishment.

After an interim of a few days—observe the temporal distancing that accompanies the stages of growing perceptiveness—the narrator and his friend, this time not by design, encounter a group of 107 camels at rest by the city wall, comfortably devouring heaps of fodder. The informant here, who speaks French well, discloses that the camels have been on the road for twenty-five days from Goulmima, to the south. (Actually Goulmima is almost due east of Marrakesh.) And that they are going no further; they are to be sold for slaughter in Marrakesh; they are enjoying their last meal. The informant volunteers the information that he served in France during World War I. At this the narrator's perception links war with the fate of the camels.

The third stage in the melding of perceptiveness and astonishment occurs, once more by design, on the next camel-market day. The narrator is again confronted by a shrieking camel, resisting a man on the other end of a rope that is drawn through its nostrils. The man is the butcher, who, according to the vaguely familiar informant, smells of camel blood, to the terror of the doomed animal. The informant, who describes how the camel will be slaughtered, proves to be the same man who explained matters at the market a week ago. Now he adds that *he* was in World War II, present at the battle of Monte Cassino (which no one has to identify as a slaughter). The authorial *I*'s integration of astonishment and perception is complete. Camels go unmentioned during the rest of his stay in the "red city"—red supposedly owing to the way the evening sun glows on the city wall—and his literary narration of the voices of Marrakesh has begun in a way that foretells the direction of the remaining tales. Not that blood will dominate the remaining tales, but voices will, and above all the narrator's growing ability to perceive and understand them, however great his astonishment at what is said or at what is happening.

In "The Souks" his impressions include the following: the language, including the body-language, of the bazaar; how there is one area of the bazaar where all the booths and stalls are given over to the making and selling of leather goods, another area for jewelers, etc.; the "guild feeling" not only of the craftsmen but also of the goods themselves. He perceives that part of the desolation in modern Western life is due to our always having everything put into our hands ready to consume, without an opportunity to see it being made. And—well known to American supermarket comparison shoppers—prices charged the poor are higher than those charged the rich.

"The Cries of the Blind" refers to the beggars' repeated cry of "Allah." To understand this requires no Arabic. But the "acoustical arabesques" wound about the repetitive sound are astounding in their phonetic variety. One gradually understands that there is seductiveness in a life given over to simple repetition. The blind beggars are "saints of repetition."

The blind marabout of "The Marabout's Saliva" is a remarkable—but at first glance astoundingly disgusting—holy man whose habit it is to chew the coins he is given and then to spit both coin and saliva into his left hand before depositing the coin into a pouch. The narrator proffers a coin, witnesses the procedure, and in his disgust gapes open-mouthed. At that, two or three pairs of eyes are trained on *him*, for his reaction is odd. He leaves. A bit of time—in this case unspecified—elapses, and perception dawns. Because the marabout is a holy man, his spittle too is holy. As such, its contact with the giver's coin confers a special blessing on the giver, over and above the reward that heaven will confer for the eleemosynary generosity. There is a third stage of perception one week later when the authorial *I* returns and gives another coin to the marabout, only to be informed by a bystander that the marabout actually chews the coin to determine its denomination. Not so; for after expectorating the coin the marabout says a blessing six times for the narrator, and the friendliness and warmth of his expression surpass anything the narrator has ever seen.

"The Silent House and the Empty Rooftops" relates the authorial *I*'s reaction to these features of the Marrakesh architectural landscape. The silent house is an essential refuge from the tumult and harshness of the city. And the rooftops—why are they empty? Can he not remain on the rooftop to glance not at the distant Atlas Mountains but at what goes on in the neighbor's courtyard? No, he is informed, and reluctantly understands, it is bad manners to notice such things, especially if there are women to be seen. One must look away. The swallows are more fortunate.

"The Woman at the Grille" presents first the visual picture, then the acoustic picture, of an oval face pressed against the window bars murmuring endearments in Arabic. The narrator, without knowing Arabic, knows that they are endearments, perhaps laced with pleading: please don't go. That is astonishing as well as pleasing. Then he is informed—or rather has his suspicion confirmed—by one of a group of happy schoolboys, a nine-year-old whom the narrator likes and thus associates with the woman at the window. "Elle est très malade, monsieur [she is very sick, sir] dans sa tête [in her head."][3] In a word, mentally ill. None of the children is laughing anymore.

In the center of *Voices,* the seventh and eighth of the fourteen tales, are "A Visit to the Mellah" and "The Dahan Family." Whereas the preceding as well as the subsequent tales are short, averaging four or five pages, the two central tales are much longer. Their importance is not only that of central position, then, but also that of dimension. Not surprisingly their contents mark a significant way station on the authorial *I*'s narrative journey to the perception of the astounding—in other words, to invoke Canetti's key concept, to his transformation. That transformation is signaled by the greater intensity of the Jewish narrator's involvement and self-identification, as well as by the greater specificity of his personal contacts.

The Mellah is the Jewish district of Marrakesh, home of tradition-encrusted, orientalized Jews of the most striking physical heterogeneity. The narrator visits a school; the children are learning the Hebrew alphabet. He encounters Jewish beggars for the first time. A young man volunteers to take him through a gate into the Jewish cemetery—although "le cimetière israélite" proves to be the extent of the guide's French vocabulary. It is a desolate open space, no grass, a vast rubble heap. But reflecting Canetti's preoccupation with surviving, with beating death, the narrator is struck by his own enviable situation. For he has survived all the people whose names are inscribed on the gravestones. Although he is loathe to admit it to himself, it is as if he had defeated each one in single combat.

The insistent beggars have followed him into the graveyard, one a heavy fellow on crutches who hurls himself at the narrator like a threatening animal. The narrator is pulled to safety by his guide. After the near-assault by the beggar, however, the desolation of the area seems no longer quite so desolate. Why? Because the assailant was "its rightful occupant." In a tiny house of prayer are more beggars, maybe fifty. The narrator, frightened but at the same time emotionally moved by "the seduction of having oneself dismembered alive for others" (52), is thinking along the lines of a sacrificial victim in *Crowds and Power*; and his verbalized thought has to be intensely personal, perhaps even more so than his inchoate identification with the Jews—beggars and all—of the Mellah.

In the Jewish barrio the authorial *I* undertakes a climactic leap from anonymity when he forms an expanding circle of acquaintanceships in the Dahan family: two brothers, a sister-in-law, an uncle, the father—"that magnificent man." There is a kind of mutual recognition scene when the one brother who can speak French suddenly asks the narrator, "Etes-vous Israélite?" (58). The latter responds with an enthusiastic yes. The brother then confides that his first name is Elie—French for Elias, as in Elias Canetti. Elie, buoyed by the felt closeness of ethnicity and nomenclature, tries to induce the narrator to write a letter of recommendation to the American commandant of Ben Guérir camp; Elie would like a job there. To the narrator, Elie's quest seems futile, but in the spirit of perceptiveness of the astounding, he obliges.

With "Storytellers and Scribes" Canctti resumes the stories of shorter length. He is on the home stretch, so to speak, of perception. Even so, the present tale ends with a question. His clear intention is to contrast the flamboyant tellers of oral tales with the disciplined professionals of the written word. The authorial *I*'s sympathy and admiration are all for the former, who, though hardly involved with the crowds of devotees who surround them, are nonetheless exposed to the noise and the hustle and bustle of their environment: life. Whereas the scribes are in comparative isolation in the quietest part of the Djema el Fna Square, and each one in turn is surrounded by space: sterility. On the basis of the perceived contrast the narrator reproaches himself for having gone over to the camp of the scribes. A splendid family of Berbers, headed by a husband obviously competent in every field but one, sit, erect and dignified, before a small scribe. What could it have been, the authorial *I* later muses, that required their joint presence before the small scribe? As if, we interpret, it were an impropriety for the representatives of a strong but illiterate oral tradition to be obliged to consult the insignificant practitioner of the written word.

"Choosing a Loaf" is the shortest sketch of all, a mere page and a half. In the evening the narrator goes to the section of Djema el Fna where women, squatting on the ground, sell bread. He compares the shapes of the various loaves to the shapes of the women who sell them. In addition to keeping the Djema el Fna before our eyes and in our minds, the tale serves to alert the narrator, to make him perceptive of the sexuality that pervades

Marrakesh. At the same time it alerts the reader to the sexuality that will pervade the stories yet to come. Men with bold looks walk past the bread sellers. One man or another might stop and test a loaf. If he should decide to buy it, he tosses a coin to the woman, and the chosen loaf disappears under the folds of his robe as he walks away.

"The Calumny"—if it is one—is perpetrated on the beggar children who gather near the Kutubiya Restaurant. (As the narrator becomes increasingly familiar with—perceptive of—Marrakesh he makes increasing use of proper names.) The perpetrator of the calumny is the proprietor of the restaurant, a Frenchman. The substance of it is that the children are prostitutes. No, replies the narrator, that can't be true. The proprietor: Oh, but it is. And he launches into a tale, in French and thus incomprehensible to the children, of how bad, how wicked things are—and of how he and two companions once did a whore out of her earnings. With that tale he sinks in the estimate of the narrator to a level far beneath that of the beggar children, whether the charge is a calumny or the truth. Most critics who express a judgment take it to be true, although Canetti himself leans in the opposite direction, not least by virtue of the title he chose for his story. With this tale *The Voices of Marrakesh* is not done with the subject of prostitution in Marrakesh. Perception is progressive, in this respect as in others.

The following tale, "The Donkey's Concupiscence," well sustains the atmosphere by now freighted with sex. The authorial *I* comes across what he judges to be the most truly miserable, abused donkey of all of Marrakesh's miserable donkeys—part of a donkey act in the Djema el Fna. Next day the narrator returns to the square. Observe the typical interim between initial astonishment and enlightened perception. Only in this case it is *re*-astonishment that precedes perception. For the aged and pitiful donkey, ill-treated too, suddenly develops a prodigious erection. The perception: the creature judged to have nothing left may have quite a bit left.

Not ten paces from the Djema el Fna is the small, all-night French bar from which the penultimate story gets its name, "Sheherazade." The proprietor is Madame Mignon; Monsieur Mignon, an ex-Legionnaire, assists her almost not at all. Madame Mignon makes extensive use of her twenty-two-year-old friend, Ginette, who habitually sits, smartly dressed and pale-complexioned, on one of the high counter stools and waits. Ginette has been born in Marrakesh of an English father and an Italian mother; the former had decamped for Dakar, leaving mother and daughter to fend for themselves. By now they are no longer in touch—but not because of any maternal disapproval of Ginette's life style. Ginette would like to visit England, but most of all she just wants out of Morocco. She is waiting for a knight errant to help her realize that goal.

She was not alone when she first attracted the narrator's attention. Beside her, as often, was a young, girlish-looking Moroccan man, with whom she drank and danced closely and exchanged caresses. With them sometimes was another man, about thirty, more masculine, less dandified. But it was the first man who was her husband, and in spite of appearances they were not on their honeymoon; they had been married a year. And to judge from her longing looks toward the door, it was not her husband for whose presence she yearned, nor for that of their companion.

A riddle, at least to the narrator, who is helped to perception by Madame Mignon. It is not a menage à trois—or rather it is that and more. Ginette's husband, the young Frenchified dandy, is the homosexual lover of the other man, who is a son of a local potentate and can pay well. The three often sleep together. In addition, Ginette's husband panders her to other men, but only those who can pay. Sometimes she refuses and is beaten by her husband. She will not take money if she likes a man, and she is beaten then as well. Not a pretty picture, and if we consider *Voices* an integrated work of art, not a series of merely interesting sketches, then we are conceivably justified in keeping the Sheherazadian prostitution in mind while we reconsider the children in "The Calumny."

What becomes of Ginette? Madame Mignon tells the narrator, whom Ginette has taken for an Englishman, thus the best of all possible saviors, that Ginette is willing to go away with him if he is willing. On no account, however, should he pay her husband money, for that would not benefit Ginette. How sweet she was a year ago! And why not?—an Englishwoman after all. The narrator: One could guess as much from her refinement. Left unsaid is his presumable perception that, at least in Morocco, he cannot be responsible for the way life is—for the way Ginette's life is, just as he cannot be responsible for that of the condemned camels in the first story.

"The Unseen" is an affecting conclusion to *The Voices of Marrakesh*. The unseen is a human being, a small brown bundle on the ground in the Djema el Fna. It continually utters a long-drawn-out "e-e-e-e-e-e-e" sound, like the buzzing of an insect. The mouth is not visible, nor the eyes, nor any part of the face. The narrator has never seen the bundle stand. He does not know where it disappears to for the rest of the night. Maybe it has no arms to reach after the coins, maybe no tongue to form the "l" of Allah. And yet the narrator, in awareness of his helplessness to change things, feels proud of the unseen, the bundle. Because it is alive, and its sound outlives all the other sounds of the city. It survives.

While the conventions of narrative time and narrative delay have led us to designate the narrator of *The Voices of Marrakesh* as the authorial *I* or the narrator, it is Canetti to whom he speaks and for whom he thinks and reflects. The themes—survival, transformation, the acoustic mask—are transparently those of Canetti. In the final story, for example, a human being is transformed into a brown bundle, the brown bundle into a sound. And the narrator is ever prepared to transform himself in each sketch, from astounded or at least bemused to perceptive, and over the course of the book from a Marrakesh visitor who is affected by the "tragic" death of camels to a more seasoned visitor who admires a mere elongated syllable as a symbol of life.

## NOTES

1. Cited by Herbert G. Göpfert (to whom the letter was addressed), "Zu den 'Stimmen von Marrakesch,'" in Stefan H. Kaszyński, ed. *Die Lesbarkeit der Welt: Elias Canettis Anthropologie und Poetik* (Poznań: Wydawnictwo Naukowe Uniwersytetu im. Adama Mickiewicza, 1984) 135.

2. Göpfert 139; Ofelia Martí Peña, " 'Die Stimmen von Marrakesch' de Elias Canetti," Roberto Corcoll and Marisa Seguán, eds. *Homenaje a Elias Canetti* (Kassel: Reichenberger, 1987) 165.

3. Elias Canetti, *The Voices of Marrakesh: A Record of a Visit*, trans. J. A. Underwood (New York: Farrar, Straus, 1984) 38. Subsequent references are noted parenthetically.

# BIBLIOGRAPHY

## Works by Elias Canetti

*Hochzeit*. Berlin: S. Fischer, 1932. [*The Wedding*. Trans. Gitta Honegger. New York: Performance Arts Journal Publications, 1986.]

*Die Blendung*. Vienna: Herbert Reichner, 1936. [*Auto-da-Fé*. Trans. C. V. Wedgwood. London: Jonathan Cape, 1946. *The Tower of Babel*. Trans. C. V. Wedgwood. New York: Stein and Day, 1947.]

*Komödie der Eitelkeit*. Munich: Willi Weismann, 1950. Frankfurt am Main: S. Fischer, 1950. [In *Comedy of Vanity and Life-Terms*. Trans. Gitta Honegger. New York: Performing Arts Journal Publications, 1983.]

*Fritz Wotruba*. Vienna: Brüder Rosenbaum, 1955.

*Masse und Macht*. Hamburg: Claassen, 1960. [*Crowds and Power*. Trans. Carol Stewart. London: Victor Gollancz, 1962; New York: Viking, 1962.]

*Welt im Kopf: Auswahl aus dem Werk* (The World in His Head: Selections from the Works). Ed. Erich Fried. Graz, Vienna: Stiasny, 1962.

*Die Befristeten*. Munich: Hanser, 1964. [In *Comedy of Vanity and Life-Terms*. Trans. Gitta Honegger. New York: Performing Arts Journal Publications, 1983. *The Numbered*. Trans. Carol Stewart. London: Marion Boyars, 1984.]

*Dramen (Hochzeit, Komödie der Eitelkeit, Die Befristeten)*. Munich: Hanser, 1964. [*The Plays of Elias Canetti (The Wedding, Comedy of Vanity, The Numbered)*. New York: Farrar, Straus, 1984.]

*Aufzeichnungen 1942–1948* (Essays 1942–1948). Munich: Hanser, 1965. Frankfurt am Main: Suhrkamp, 1965.

*Die Stimmen von Marrakesch: Aufzeichnungen nach einer Reise*. Munich: Hanser, 1967. [*The Voices of Marrakesh: A Record of a Visit*. Trans. J. A. Underwood. London: Marion Boyars, 1978. New York: Seabury, 1978.]

*Der andere Prozess: Kafkas Briefe an Felice*. Munich: Hanser, 1969. [*Kafka's Other Trial: The Letters to Felice*. Trans. Christopher Middleton. London: Calder and Boyars, 1975. New York: Schocken, 1978.]

*Alle vergeudete Verehrung: Aufzeichnungen 1949–1960*. (All Wasted Veneration: Essays 1949–1960) Munich: Hanser, 1970.

*Die gespaltene Zukunft: Aufsätze und Gespräche*. (The Sundered Future: Essays and Conversations) Munich: Hanser, 1972.

*Macht und Überleben: Drei Essays* (Power and Survival: Three Essays). Berlin: Literarisches Colloquium, 1972.

*Die Provinz des Menschen: Aufzeichnungen 1942–1972.* Munich: Hanser, 1973. [*The Human Province.* Trans. Joachim Neugroschel. New York: Seabury, 1978.]
*Der Ohrenzeuge: Fünfzig Charaktere.* Munich: Hanser, 1974. [*Earwitness: Fifty Characters.* Trans. Joachim Neugroschel. New York: Seabury, 1979.]
*Der Überlebende* (The Survivor). Frankfurt am Main: Suhrkamp, 1975.
*Das Gewissen der Worte: Essays.* Munich: Hanser, 1975. [*The Conscience of Words.* Trans. Joachim Neugroschel. New York: Seabury, 1979.]
*Die gerettete Zunge: Geschichte einer Jugend.* Munich: Hanser, 1977. [*The Tongue Set Free: Remembrance of a European Childhood.* Trans. Joachim Neugroschel. New York: Seabury, 1980.]
*Die Fackel im Ohr: Lebensgeschichte 1921–1931.* Munich: Hanser, 1980. [*The Torch in My Ear.* Trans. Joachim Neugroschel. New York: Farrar, Straus, 1982.]
*Das Augenspiel: Lebensgeschichte 1931–1937.* Munich: Hanser, 1985. [*The Play of the Eyes.* Trans. Ralph Manheim. New York: Farrar, Straus, 1986.]
*Das Geheimherz der Uhr: Aufzeichnungen 1973–1985.* Munich: Hanser, 1987. [*The Secret Heart of the Clock: Notes, Aphorisms, Fragments, 1973–1985.* Trans. Joel Agee. New York: Farrar, Straus, 1989.]

**BIBLIOGRAPHIES**

Ciacchi, Mara, et al. "Bibliografia Elias Canetti." *Nuovi Argomenti* 40/41/42 (1975): 400–09.
Dissinger, Dieter. In Herbert G. Göpfert, ed. *Canetti lesen: Erfahrungen mit seinen Büchern.* Munich: Hanser, 1975. 136–66.
Jung, Werner, and Sibylle Späth. "Bibliographie zu Elias Canetti." *Text + Kritik* 28 (1982): 76–86.
Périsson-Waldmüller, Jutta. "Bibliographie générale." *Austriaca* 11 (1980): 165–86.
Stieg, Gerald. "Canetti en France." *Austriaca* 12 (1981): 209–10. [Continuation of bibliography in vol. 11.]
————. "Kommentierte Auswahlbibliographie." *Zu Elias Canetti.* Ed. Manfred Durzak. Stuttgart: Klett, 1983. 171–80.

**CRITICAL WORKS**

Arnold, Heinz Ludwig, ed. "Elias Canetti." *Text + Kritik* 28 (1970). Stuttgart: Boorberg. Successor editions in 1973 and 1982. Worthwhile collections of essays.
Aspetsberger, Friedbert, and Gerald Stieg, eds. *Elias Canetti: Blendung als Lebensform.* Königstein/Ts.: Athenäum, 1985. A good collection of essays relating to *Auto-da-Fé.*
Barnouw, Dagmar. *Elias Canetti.* Stuttgart: Metzler, 1979. A useful handbook to Canetti's works with emphasis, even overemphasis, on *Crowds and Power.* In-

cludes a good bibliography up to 1979, although not without scattered mistakes. Although it lacks historical perspective, it is a good critical starting point.

Bartsch, Kurt, and Gerhard Melzer, eds. *Experte der Macht, Elias Canetti*. Graz: Droschl, 1985. Essays on power and survivorship in Canetti.

Bischoff, Alfons-M. *Elias Canetti: Stationen zum Werk*. Bern: Herbert Lang, 1973; Frankfurt am Main: Peter Lang, 1973. Includes a good bibliography, arranged by years, through 1969. The text should be read with great caution, however, for it has become dated. In any case, it steers clear of *Crowds and Power*.

Corcoll, Roberto, and Marisa Siguán, eds. *Homenaje a Elias Canetti*. Kassel: Reichenberger, 1987. A collection of essays mostly by Catalan scholars. The essays range from the ordinary to the highly insightful. For readers of Spanish, a very useful book. Abstracts in English. Bibliography gives current rather than first editions of Canetti's works, but it is good for secondary literature.

Curtius, Mechtild. *Kritik der Verdinglichung in Canettis Roman "Die Blendung": Eine sozialpsychologische Literaturanalyse*. Bonn: Bouvier, 1973. A significant monograph on *Auto-da-Fé* from a Freudian and Marxist perspective. Not for those just getting acquainted with *Auto-da-Fé*.

Darby, David. *Structures of Disintegration: Narrative Strategies in Elias Canetti's "Die Blendung."* Riverside, CA: Ariadne, 1991. An excellent monograph that frees *Auto-da-Fé* and its narrative strategies from dependence on *Crowds and Power*.

Daviau, Donald G., ed. Special issue of *Modern Austrian Literature* 16, nos. 3/4 (1983). A fine collection of essays, largely but not entirely on *Auto-da-Fé* and *Crowds and Power*. About half of the essays are in English.

Dissinger, Dieter. *Vereinzelung und Massenwahn: Elias Canettis Roman "Die Blendung."* Bonn: Bouvier, 1971. A monograph that attempts to explicate *Auto-da-Fé* on the basis of its language and the supposed fundamentality to it of *Crowds and Power*.

Durzak, Manfred, ed. *Zu Elias Canetti*. Stuttgart: Klett, 1983. A well-written group of essays covering many aspects of Canetti's work. Indispensable for the serious student. Contains a select bibliography.

Eigler, Friederike. *Das autobiographische Werk von Elias Canetti*. Tübingen: Stauffenburg, 1988. An excellent monograph dwelling on Canetti's autobiographical works. Original insights. Presumes a substantial literary-historical background.

Fendel, Hildegard. *Die Sicht des Todes bei Elias Canetti und seine Fragen an die Theologie*. Göttingen: Verein für Wissenschaftliches Schrifttum, 1986. Canetti's view of death and the theological questions raised thereby.

Feth, Hans. *Elias Canettis Dramen*. Frankfurt am Main: R. G. Fischer, 1980. A thorough discussion of Canetti's plays, but not methodologically consistent in its approach.

Göpfert, Herbert G., ed. *Canetti lesen: Erfahrungen mit seinen Büchern.* Munich: Hanser, 1975. A collection of essays edited by the chief editor at Canetti's longtime publisher.

Hennighaus, Lothar. *Tod und Verwandlung: Elias Canettis poetische Anthropologie aus der Kritik der Psychoanalyse.* Frankfurt am Main: Peter Lang, 1984. A psychoanalytic perspective on Canetti's "poetic anthropology" with attention to his doctrine of transformation. An essential book for those interested in psychoanalytic perspectives on Canetti.

*Hüter der Verwandlung: Beiträge zum Werk Elias Canettis.* Munich: Hanser, 1985. A collection of first-rate essays published in honor of Canetti's eightieth birthday. [*Essays in Honor of Elias Canetti.* Trans. Michael Hulse. New York: Farrar, Straus, 1987. Highly recommended.]

Kaszyński, Stefan H., ed. *Die Lesbarkeit der Welt: Elias Canettis Anthropologie und Poetik.* Poznań: Wdawnictwo Naukowe Uniwersytetu im. Adama Mickiewicza, 1984. Although published in Poland, all of the essays in this collection are in German. The several aspects of Canetti are well represented.

Krumme, Detlef. *Lesemodelle: Elias Canetti ("Die Blendung"), Günter Grass ("Die Blechtrommel"), Walter Höllerer ("Elephantenuhr").* Munich: Hanser, 1983. Possibly the best of a number of books that bring Canetti into comparison with other writers.

Meili, Barbara. *Erinnerung und Vision: Der lebensgeschichtliche Hintergrund von Elias Canettis Roman "Die Blendung."* Bonn: Bouvier, 1985. A well-written monograph on the autobiographical background in *Auto-da-Fé.*

Moser, Manfred. *Musil, Canetti, Eco, Calvino: Die überholte Philosophie.* Vienna: Verband der Wissenschaftlichen Gesellschaften Österreichs, 1986. Comparison on a philosophical basis.

Piel, Edgar. *Elias Canetti.* Munich: C. H. Beck, Edition Text + Kritik, 1984. A useful handbook for the beginner.

Powe, B. W. *The Solitary Outlaw.* Toronto: Lester and Orpen Dennys, 1987. An original perspective on Canetti. Useful.

Roberts, David. *Kopf und Welt: Elias Canettis Roman "Die Blendung."* Munich: Hanser, 1975. A very readable retelling, interpretation, and discussion of *Auto-da-Fé. Crowds and Power* is used with caution to help explain the novel.

Széll, Szusza. *Ichverlust und Scheingemeinschaft: Das Gesellschaftsbild in den Romanen von Kafka, Musil, Broch, Canetti, Saiko.* Budapest: Akademie, 1979. The loss of personal identity and the factitious social structure in the novels of several authors, including Canetti. Locates Canetti culturally and historically.

**SELECT BIBLIOGRAPHY OF ARTICLES IN ENGLISH**

Barnouw, Dagmar. "Doubting Death: On Elias Canetti's Drama *The Deadlined* [The Numbered]." *Mosaic* 7.2 (1974): 1–23.

Beller, Manfred. "The Fire of Prometheus and the Theme of Progress in Goethe, Nietzsche, Kafka, and Canetti." *College Literature* 17.1–2 (1984): 1–13.

Cohen, Yaier. "Elias Canetti: Exile and the German Language." *German Life and Letters* 42 (1988–89): 32–45.

Darby, David. "A Fiction of Detection: The Police Enquiry in Elias Canetti's *Auto-da-Fé*." *Semiotics 1988*. Ed. Terry Prewitt, John Deely, and Karen Haworth. Lanham, MD: University Press of America, 1989. 343–49.

Düssel, Reinhard. "Aspects of Confucianism in Elias Canetti's Notes and Essays." *Tamkang Review* 18.1–4 (1987–88): 333–41.

Gould, Robert. "*Die gerettete Zunge* and *Dichtung und Wahrheit:* Hypertextuality in Autobiography and Its Implications." *Seminar* 21 (1985): 79–107.

Honegger, Gitta. "Acoustic Masks: Strategies of Language in the Theater of Canetti, Bernhard, and Handke." *Modern Austrian Literature* 18.2 (1985): 57–66.

Kimball, Roger. "Becoming Elias Canetti." *New Criterion* 5.1 (1986): 17–28.

Rosenfeld, Sidney. "1981 Nobel Laureate Elias Canetti: A Writer Apart." *World Literature Today* 56.1 (1982): 5–9.

Russell, Peter. "The Vision of Man in Elias Canetti's *Die Blendung*." *German Life and Letters* 28 (1974–75): 24–35.

Sacharoff, Mark. "Grotesque Comedy in Canetti's *Auto da Fe*." *Critique* 14.1 (1972): 99–112.

Seidler, Ingo. "Who Is Elias Canetti?" *Cross Currents: A Yearbook of Central European Culture* 1982: 107–23.

Sokel, Walter H. "The Ambiguity of Madness: Elias Canetti's Novel *Die Blendung*." *Views and Reviews of Modern German Literature: Festschrift für Adolf D. Klarmann*. Ed. Karl S. Weimar. Englewood Cliffs, NJ: Prentice-Hall, 1974. 181–87.

Sontag, Susan. "Mind as Passion." *Under the Sign of Saturn*. New York: Farrar, Straus, 1980. 181–204.

Stenberg, Peter. "Remembering Times Past: Canetti, Sperber, and 'A World That Is No More'." *Seminar* 17 (1981): 296–311.

Thompson, Edward. "Elias Canetti's *Die Blendung* and the Changing Image of Madness." *German Life and Letters* 26 (1972–73): 38–47.

Thorpe, Kathleen. "Notes on 'Die Blendung' by Elias Canetti." *Theoria* 67 (1986): 61–67.

Turner, David. "Elias Canetti: The Intellectual as King Canute." *Modern Austrian Writing: Literature and Society after 1945*. Ed. Alan Best and Hans Wolfschütz. London: Wolff; Totowa, NJ: Barnes and Noble, 1980. 79–96.

Wiley, Marion E. "Elias Canetti's Reflective Prose." *Modern Austrian Literature* 12.2 (1979): 129–39.

# INDEX

The index does not include references to material in the notes.